GROUP DYNAMICS FOR
HIGH-RISK TEAMS

GROUP DYNAMICS FOR HIGH-RISK TEAMS

▼

A 'TEAM RESOURCE MANAGEMENT' (TRM) PRIMER

AMY L. FRAHER, EdD

iUniverse, Inc.

New York Lincoln Shanghai

Group Dynamics for High-Risk Teams
A 'Team Resource Management' (TRM) Primer

Copyright © 2005 by Amy L. Fraher

iUniverse books may be ordered through booksellers or by contacting:

iUniverse
2021 Pine Lake Road, Suite 100
Lincoln, NE 68512
www.iuniverse.com
1-800-Authors (1-800-288-4677)

ISBN-13: 978-0-595-37739-8 (pbk)
ISBN-13: 978-0-595-82118-1 (ebk)
ISBN-10: 0-595-37739-4 (pbk)
ISBN-10: 0-595-82118-9 (ebk)

Printed in the United States of America

For information contact:

Amy L. Fraher, EdD

Chief Pilot
Aviation Operations Program
San Diego Miramar College
10440 Black Mountain Road
San Diego, CA 92126-2999
USA
(619) 388-7664
afraher@sdccd.net
www.sdmiramar.edu/programs/avia

Director and Principal Consultant
Paradox and Company
4704 Miracle Drive
San Diego, CA 92115
USA
amy@paradoxandcompany.com
www.paradoxandcompany.com

Acknowledgments

As with any project of this magnitude, many people and organizations have been influential in its creation. Some, such as my colleagues at the Tavistock Institute of Human Relations, International Society for the Psychoanalytic Study of Organizations (ISPSO) and An Organisation for Promoting Understanding in Society (OPUS) provided me with intellectual stimulation, a forum to exchange ideas and test my theories through their scholarly activities. Others provided invaluable experiential learning opportunities at their Tavistock-based group relations events such as the Tavistock Institute's *Leicester Conference*, University of San Diego's doctoral program and the A.K. Rice Institute for the Study of Social Systems and its Affiliates such as Grex and Washington-Baltimore Center. In addition many authors have written brilliantly about group study over the years, providing innumerable influential insights which have underpinned many theories within this book. I would like to thank them all for their contributions to this *Primer*.

I would also like to thank my colleagues Clare Doherty, Miguel Guilarte, Karen Izod, Ross Lazar, Mannie Sher, Phil Swann, Janedra Sykes and my editor, Kathleen B. Jones, for their support and encouragement of my research, writing and study of groups.

Finally, thanks to my colleagues at San Diego Miramar College, in particular the dean, faculty, staff and students of the *School of Technical Careers and Work Force Initiatives* who provided invaluable assistance in the development of this *Team Resource Management* model.

☙ Contents

CHAPTER I

▼

AN INTRODUCTION

 *LEARNING OBJECTIVES*

> 1. Identify the roots of *Team Resource Management (TRM)*.
> 2. Clarify the definition of a high-risk team.
> 3. Explain why high-risk teams differ from other groups.

Group Dynamics for High-Risk Teams is a *Team Resource Management (TRM) Primer* designed to introduce a new team building model called *TRM* and serves as a guide for experiential learning events based in the Tavistock tradition. Using examples from popular culture as well as industry case studies, this *Primer* helps the reader explore the application of concepts such as leadership, management, authority, role, task, boundaries and teamwork in high-risk teams.

The roots of *TRM* can be traced to the theories and methods of 1) The Tavistock approach to group study; 2) *Crew Resource Management (CRM)* from the field of aviation; and 3) my own twenty years of leadership experience, first as an enlisted Marine, then Naval Officer, Naval Aviator, flight instructor, commercial airline pilot, social scientist and college professor.

The influence of these three areas will become clear as we explore *leader-ship, authority* and *teamwork* in the following chapters.[1]

What is a *high-risk* team? For our purposes, *a high-risk team is two or more people working together in an environment where there is significant risk of injury or death to themselves or to others as a result of their per-formance.* Professionals in fields such as aviation, military, law enforce-ment and firefighting risk their own personal safety at work every day, making these excellent examples of *high-risk* professions. Other fields such as automotive technology, emergency planning, engineering, medicine, nuclear power or off-shore drilling, among others, may not seem as risky for individuals working within them, yet decisions and actions made by people in these fields can greatly affect the safety of others. Just imagine yourself on the operating table—the surgeon and his or her team's safety may not be directly at risk, but your health certainly is. Therefore, we will consider these *high-risk teams* as well.

Why focus on high-risk teams? All groups and organizations have subtle, and not so subtle, dynamics that influence team behavior and perform-ance. Yet, teams operating in stressful environments, such as those listed above, also have unique characteristics determined both by the nature of their tasks and their hazardous operating environments. These include *fac-tors such time urgency, peer pressure, exposure to personal risk, professional competitiveness, interpersonal conflicts, reputation management and liv-ing with the weighty repercussions of one's decisions, which often combine to make decision-making in high-risk teams a stressful activity.*

Little research has been conducted on the unique dynamics high-risk groups must manage in their teams' operations. Although other team models exist, exploring how professionals in high-risk fields might increase their awareness of: **1) the dynamics of authority relations; 2) factors affecting the *act of authorizing*; and 3) the interdependent nature of leadership, while 4) assisting participants to learn how to manage anxi-ety and continue to think and function in stressful situations** only recently has been undertaken. This *Primer* and the experiential exercises that go along with it fill this gap by offering participants the opportunity to examine these important issues, deciding for themselves what is relevant and applicable in their work environment. Understanding the internal dynamics of groups and teams will allow participants to become more effective leaders, followers and teammates who are better able to analyze factors impacting the success or failure of team efforts.

▼

CHAPTER II

LEADERSHIP IN HIGH-RISK TEAMS[2]

 *LEARNING OBJECTIVES*

1. Describe how a crowd is different from a group.
2. Identify the five characteristics that differentiate a team from a group.
3. Explain how leadership and management differ.
4. Clarify the definition of authority and the *act of authorizing*.
5. Distinguish between *formal authority roles* and *informal authority roles*.
6. Explain why participating in groups often causes anxiety.

Introduction

Successful leaders in today's business, management and technical fields know that leadership requires more than vision, charisma, technical competence or mechanical proficiency. Many recent studies[3] provide evidence from "a number of high-hazard, high-reliability industries," such as aviation, medicine, and nuclear power, "showing how failures of communication, poor teamwork and poor leadership are common human factors precursors to accidents," loss of life and damage to equipment.[4] In order to exercise leadership effectively—even in such highly specialized areas as aviation, automotive technology, computer science, emergency planning, medicine, off-shore drilling, military, law enforcement and firefighting—professionals today must acquire an understanding of *individual psychology, group dynamics* and the impact of *systemic* influences.[5] This *Primer* will introduce you to these topics.

Not since World War II has the world been challenged by emergencies and devastation as it has in the last half-decade. Severe flooding in the United Kingdom in 2000, terrorist attacks in New York and Washington DC in 2001, ongoing insurgency in the Middle East, Egypt, Turkey and Iraq, bombings in Madrid in 2004 and London in 2005, the Tsunami in Asia in 2004, Hurricane Katrina and Rita in New Orleans, floods in Guatemala, and the Pakistani earthquake in 2005, just to name a few, have challenged governments, emergency planners, transportation officials, law enforcement officers, fire fighters, armed forces, and emergency medical services to operate in innovative and collaborative ways on short notice.

Without exception, industry experts describe the post-9/11 world as a *new operating environment,* increasing demands for better communication, collaboration, team-building expertise and peer mentoring. For example, 9/11 in New York taught us that law enforcement teams need to collaborate with fire fighters, ambulance paramedics, politicians, and emergency response teams within the transportation system. On 7/7 in London, we saw excellent examples of this increased collaboration. As a result, both casualties and chaos were contained.

Since 7/7, police chiefs from around the US have been working to create "an informal network" for more "rapid communication…They [also] hope to work with police forces in Europe, the Middle East and Asia to share information."[6] This new operating environment requires knowledge and skills beyond the technical ones traditionally taught in professional programs. To succeed, it is no longer enough to achieve technical competence; one must develop the awareness, skills, and behaviors necessary for safe and efficient operation in today's increasingly dynamic environments.

This new, more *present* leadership model supports leaders to communicate across many different boundaries, manage themselves in multiple roles, and hone reflective capabilities using what has been called *emotional intelligence* to inform actions. When leaders understand and mange their emotions research shows that they become better able to respond flexibly, consider alternative scenarios and make decisions by using emotions as signals to prioritize demands.[7] By understanding how *authority* dynamics affect formal and informal leadership roles such leaders are better able to manage resistance to change. We will discuss these points further later.

In fact, research has shown that "in leadership positions, almost 90 percent of the competencies necessary for success are social and emotional in nature."[8] Emotional intelligence skills such as the ability to stay motivated, face frustration, control impulses, manage anxiety and "keep distress from swamping the ability to think"[9] become critical to decisionmaking under conditions of stress. Some experts claim that these skills "can be as powerful, and at times more powerful, than IQ" as a determinant of successful job performance.[10]

Yet, emotional intelligence largely has been overlooked in leadership and team training. Once "considered an oxymoron by some" because "emotions convey the idea of unreasonableness,"[11] new brain research reveals the emotional and cognitive centers of the brain to be far more integrated than previously thought. And, important for the development of team training, these "crucial emotional competencies can indeed be learned."[12]

Understanding the emotional intelligence of a group's leader as not simply an *individual's* leadership characteristic, but as having "a powerful impact on the *group's* climate and effectiveness"[13] is important. Although the leader and group share a powerfully interdependent relationship, the emotionally intelligent leader understands "group, intergroup and organizational dynamics, particularly as they affect emotional functioning, and [is] skillful in working with those dynamics."[14] Leaders must learn to comprehend and manage emotions, develop the confidence to take action on the basis of this understanding and tolerate uncertainty while managing the consequences. Even leaders in highly specialized and technical fields can—and should—develop skills of observation, analysis and reflection in order to increase their job performance.

This *Primer* outlines the research behind and principles of an *experiential* learning program that can provide participants with an opportunity to increase their awareness of this leadership process by considering the influence of *individual psychology, group dynamics* and *systemic* factors, such as organizational, social and environmental elements, on human behavior. Understanding the internal dynamics of groups and teams will help participants become more effective leaders, followers and teammates who use resources more efficiently.

Teamwork is not something one learns simply by reading about it. Like any new skill, after preliminary instruction, one must practice in order to develop appropriate mastery. This experiential program provides participants with *group events* or opportunities to create a '*temporary organization*' in which to **study group dynamics**—their own behavior and that of those around them—and to experiment with different work experiences and leadership roles. We will discuss this topic in more detail later.

These events are not didactic, but rather *experiential* exercises designed to **provide opportunities for learning.** Participants and event staff work together to examine what is **really going on** in the **here-and-now,** exploring the obvious or overt and not-so-obvious or covert dynamics of the organization they create together. As the name might infer, the aim of **here-and-now** events is to explore the group's behavior as it happens, focusing analysis on what is actively occurring. **Here-and-now** observations such as "no male group members have spoken in the past hour" or "there is an empty seat across from the consultant" are invitations to consider what this behavior might mean.

Just like any organization in which you have been a member, this '*temporary organization*' will develop its own culture, rituals, rules, myths and fantasies. By analyzing and interpreting their responses to different experiences, participants use their own authority to accept what is useful learning for them and reject what is not. **There are no right or wrong answers.** Throughout this process, participants can consider ways in which they gain and lose power as they exercise their authority, reproducing situations in a controlled environment, similar to everyday life. The *'temporary organization'* offers them the opportunity to experiment and react differently, without the fear of reprisal they might feel on the job in their real organizations.

While some approaches to group study[15] focus on individual behavior, a different approach emerged in the post-World War II period at the Tavistock Institute of Human Relations[16] in the United Kingdom and was subsequently termed the *Tavistock method*.[17] Central to the Tavistock method of group study is analysis of the *group's behavior as a whole*. As a result, the Tavistock approach considers the individual group member *only* as a representative of the entire group, manifesting something on behalf of the *group-as-a-whole*. We will explore this area further in subsequent chapters. For now, let us begin by becoming familiar with some new terminology.

Definition of Terms

Individuals, Crowds, Groups and *Teams*

Is there a difference between a *crowd* of individuals, a *group* of people and a *team*? Social scientists disagree and, as a result, there are a variety of perspectives about the differences. For our purposes, **an informal assembly of two or more individuals—such as you might find waiting at a bus stop, walking down a city street or passing through an airport—will be called a** *crowd*. **In a crowd, people are predominantly concerned about themselves, their own needs and satisfying their individual desires.**

This aggregate cluster of people becomes a *group* **when members interact, increasing their awareness of their inter-relatedness and dependence on one another as a common task emerges.**[18] In the examples above, a *crowd* might become a *group* when individuals line up to pay and board the bus; stop on the street to help a lost tourist with directions; or organize themselves to go through airport security screening, thereby interacting and developing a common relationship and task. This interaction need not be verbal; it might be conveyed via body language or a sequence of behaviors. Shortly after accomplishing its task, the group might transition back to being a crowd as individuals resume pursuing their own needs and desires.

The Tavistock approach hypothesizes that when this "aggregate becomes a *group*, the group behaves as a *system* "—an entity in itself, greater than the sum of its parts"—interacting with its environment.[19] Thinking about this *group-as-a-whole* requires a perceptual shift away from viewing people as distinct individuals—in control of their destiny and individual goals—to viewing them as interrelated group members, whose collective interactions tell us "something more"[20] about the *group as a system.*

Through this lens, we can see the group as a powerful force, developing a virtual *life of its own* as a consequence of the ideas and beliefs its members bring to it. In other words, whatever behavior occurs within the group, whatever members speak about in the group, is a *reflection of the group*—and not only of the individuals who are acting or speaking. In addition, the primary task of the group is survival. Therefore, the group will do whatever it takes to survive, using group members at will in service of this task.[21]

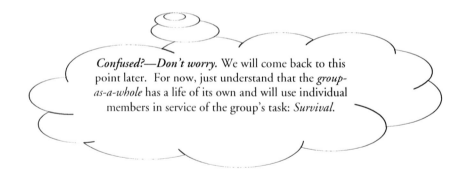

Confused?—Don't worry. We will come back to this point later. For now, just understand that the *group-as-a-whole* has a life of its own and will use individual members in service of the group's task: *Survival.*

Groups versus Teams

The distinction between *groups* and *teams* is not always as clear as that between *crowds* and *groups*. For our purposes, we will call a group a team when they:

- Commit to a *vision* or *primary task*;
- Recognize there is a collective, interdependent dimension to their relationship;
- Organize themselves in a systemic way;
- Possess authority to act on the team's behalf; and
- Share leadership roles.

Some Examples

Although there are many examples of teams in all types of organizations today, an athletic team is a good place to begin our analysis. Let us consider the San Diego *Chargers*. As a National Football League team, they share a collective team *vision* or *primary task*: Making money by winning football games.

Although the team may have other tasks such as setting records, speaking with television sportscasters, attracting new players or signing autographs for fans, the *primary task* is to win games. If they do not win, the organization will not survive. Each member of the team, from quarterback to linemen to kicker, is in support of this vision and understands that their *team will not survive* if they do not work together in a collective, interdependent manner. As a result, the team organizes itself systemically through assigned positions, team events, training rituals and game schedules. And in their various roles, as quarterback, kicker or coach, for instance, they are authorized to perform on behalf of the team, sharing *leadership roles* as a result.

Other examples of teams may not be as clear-cut. Let us consider a group dynamics event, such as this *experiential* learning environment. Individuals read a catalog or description online, register for the event and arrive at the first session. They receive a syllabus describing the event, make an assessment of the instructor and look around the room sizing up their fellow students. Many may be unsure if this event is for them, wondering "will I learn anything," "will I do well," and "is this event worth my time and money?" At this point, individuals may be behaving like a *crowd*: *Predominantly interested in satisfying their own needs and desires.*

During the first meeting, the instructor reviews the syllabus emphasizing the purpose and objectives of the event and facilitates an open discussion. Perhaps individuals begin to interact in a lively way, excited about the upcoming event. Some members start to form a *group* as they interact and develop a common relationship and task. Others may be reluctant to join so quickly, preferring the anonymity of the *crowd* instead.

At the second meeting, perhaps the instructor distributes a graded in-class exercise with a time limit of one hour and assigns people to groups of five. At first, the *crowd* is unsure of themselves and unclear about the goals of the exercise; they have difficulty locating their group in the room and worry about how they will be *individually* graded in this *team* exercise.

Example #1: After a few minutes, some groups observe that if they do not get started with the exercise they will run out of time and perhaps get a failing grade. They realize, for their *group to survive*, they need to contain their personal needs and desires and attempt the task of the exercise. Members of these groups interact with each other and agree to commit to the vision of doing the best they can on the exercise. They recognize there is a collective, interdependent dimension to their relationship: If the group fails in the task, they will each fail. One person points out that since time is limited, they must divide the tasks, organizing themselves in a systemic way. After discussing each section, they decide to empower each individual with authority to act on the team's behalf by answering separate sections of the exercise questionnaire. As different challenges arise, this group allows the most qualified member to take charge, emerging organically, as they share the leadership role. This group becomes a *team* over the course of the exercise.

Example #2: Meanwhile, another group remains reluctant to get started on the exercise. Two vocal members make their frustrations known: They are unhappy with risking their grade on the performance of their fellow students. They continue to argue about the purpose of the exercise and the best way to divide up the tasks as the rest of the group falls silent. No one seems able to agree, nor to authorize any individual to exercise leadership in order get the group on track to completing the exercise in time. Every time someone attempts to introduce a solution, they become attacked by other group members who just seem to want to argue. With just minutes left, one student grabs the questionnaire and begins writing furiously. Unfortunately time is up and they turn in a half-finished paper.

Why is this important?

At this point you may be wondering: Why is it important to differenti-ate between *crowds, groups* and *teams* in order to understand leadership, authority and teamwork better in organizational life? To answer this ques-tion fully, we must first have a working understanding of the definitions of *leadership, authority* and *role* and how these phenomena can influence peo-ple's behavior. The following section addresses these areas. So hold onto that question because it's a good one!

Leadership

Leadership is a topic which most people believe is important yet little is really understood about it. "By all counts, leadership ranks among the most researched and debated topics in the organizational sciences."[22] Yet over the past century, scholars have attempted to define *leadership* without much sense of agreement. Among the earliest sources shaping traditional definitions of leadership was Machiavelli's 16th century work entitled *The Prince*. Although Machiavelli never used the word *leadership*, he endorsed the idea of *princely rule* as an orchestration of specific acts by a talented individual in a power position designed to solicit a specific intended result. In this foundational book, Machiavelli posed the infamous leadership question: *Is it better to be loved or feared?*

Other examples of leadership theories developed over the years include ***great man, traits, behaviorist,*** and ***situational.*** At the turn of the twentieth century, ***great man theory*** espoused that only a few great men—not often women[23]—had the correct combination of natural-born skills to become leaders. It postulated that people could not learn leadership skills, they were just born with them.

A more egalitarian view of leadership emerged during the Great Depression. Rather than emphasizing natural-born characteristics, specific leadership *traits* were identified as critical. After World War II, *trait* lead-ership was replaced by ***behaviorists*** who identified specific acts as essential for effective leadership and later researchers concluded that leaders were really people who do the *right* thing in *key **situations***.

In the mid-1960s James McGregor developed his ***Theory X-Theory Y*** philosophies, echoing Machiavelli's observation of the pervasive love-hate relationship between managers and workers. McGregor was highly influenced by Elton Mayo's now famous worker efficiency study at the Hawthorne plant of the Western Electric Company in Chicago between 1927 and 1932. By studying women assembling telephone relays, Mayo explored the relationship between the worker and her work environment and the link between human motivation and productivity, paving the way for new theories which recognized organizations as complex interdependent systems.[24]

Building on this premise, McGregor's ***Theory X*** assumed that most workers prefer to be directed, are not ambitious, and must be closely monitored by management in order to achieve organizational goals. In contrast, McGregor's ***Theory Y*** offered a more integrated view of individual and organizational goals. It supposed workers are not naturally lazy or unreliable and, conditions permitting, work can be as natural as child's play. In the proper environment, people can become self-directed, creative problem-solvers who can best accomplish organizational goals by directing their own efforts.

McGregor suggested that management's task is to unleash each worker's creative potential by fostering a motivating environment through effective leadership strategies.[25] One can see traces of McGregor's *Theory Y* perspective underpinning many internet companies' efforts to design a workplace where employees can relax, play games and feel at home in an environment that fosters creativity.

Leadership versus *Management* in Today's Organizations

It was not until the mid-20th century that the term ***leadership*** actually came into vogue, and even then it was often used synonymously with ***management***. Over the past few decades, many authors have wrestled with the complex task of defining leadership, often contributing quickly fading buzz-word theories based on certain observable personality traits or inherent characteristics of *greatness*—usually based on a male model. Questions such as the following arose: Are leaders born or made? Is leadership a certain core set of skills and traits or is it a relationship between people? Will leadership in the future require the same basic abilities as it does today?[26]

One commonality among many of the more recent definitions is that leadership is understood as a sort of *influence relationship* in which *leaders induce followers to act in mutually beneficial ways*.[27] These types of influence-oriented perspectives have become commonplace as dozens of different definitions of leadership have emerged in recent years.[28]

Although it remains clear that the changing demographics, cultures, and structure of contemporary workplaces combine to challenge traditional views of hierarchical leadership models, these influence-oriented models of leadership can still come up short. Even if one were to agree with their definitions, most theories remain silent about the *process* by which a leader might achieve this *influence-relationship*. As a result, *the perennial challenge is to understand the process of leadership.*

Today, most leadership scholars make a clear distinction between leadership and management. Although leaders do manage, and managers do lead, it is commonly held that *leaders provide vision* for the future of a group, team or organization while *managers focus on the day to day* requirements of the present situation. Leaders keep the group focused on the dynamic group-leader vision of the future. Managers monitor the bottom-line, maintain the status-quo and organize resources to use current assets effectively.

Yet, because the future is invariably uncertain, leaders also must possess reflective capabilities, emotional intelligence and the ability to instill confidence so that followers invest in his or her vision. As a result, she or he often balances on a razor's edge between autonomy and dependency, rational and non-rational decision making, and realities and fantasies within the group. Examining these issues is the key element of the Tavistock method and will be taken up in subsequent chapters.

Why does understanding myths and fantasies, as well as rational decision-making, matter to the study of leadership? Because fantasies can have a critical impact on our organizational life. For instance, many theorists have "observed that, in leading others, leaders run the risk of becoming trapped in delusions of grandeur and omnipotence, fueled by narcissism. Such leaders become so absorbed in their fantasies of success and power that they lose touch with reality."[29] And since their followers have bought into the leaders' vision, questioning the leader's judgment or vision becomes tantamount to betrayal. Even if the leader is willing to abandon his or her vision, followers often are not. As a result, followers now "play a special role: Protecting the leader from reality so that the leader's faith in the vision is never threatened."[30] Organizations and teams operating in this mode often insulate themselves against reality, disregarding all signs of imminent disaster as they march blissfully toward their doom.[31]

Why think about leadership as a dynamic process? Because leadership may or may not be vested in the *designated* leader. In other words, although one person may be formally *in charge*, it might be common knowledge within the organization that the vision for the future of the organization or plan for long-term survival is held by someone else. During periods of organizational transformation, leaders often emerge with critical skills required during transition to be replaced by leaders with different skills once the transformation has occurred.

Authority

In every day language, people often use the terms **leadership** and **authority** interchangeably, similar to the interchange of leadership and management. For our purposes, we will define **authority as power legitimated by a team in an individual to perform a service on its behalf.**

Employing this definition, we see that during the **act of authorizing** two aspects become distinct:

- First, authority emerges through a leader-follower exchange of trust and power;
- Second, authority emerges—and can disappear—if this delicate trust-power exchange is violated.[32]

In other words during the *act of authorizing*, followers judge leaders' capabilities, evaluating whether to exchange trust and power or not.

Interestingly, evaluation criteria may have little foundation in actual job qualifications or performance. Many of the criteria used are unconscious and emotional in nature. For instance, demographic information such as race, gender, sexual orientation, religion, age, height, weight, attractiveness, family connections, friendships and a list of other factors, all become influential during the *act of authorizing*.

Using this definition of authority also makes it clear that, there are two types of authority: *formal* and *informal* authority. *Formal authority is constituted through roles in structured organizational settings with clearly designated leaders.* Examples of formal authority can be found in the military, government, and law enforcement where these organizations demand that subordinates confer their commanders with power and trust simply because of their rank and assigned jobs.

By contrast, *informal authority is constituted through personal attributes that instill a sense of confidence in followers who confer trust and power on someone to act on their behalf.* Therefore, informal authority is awarded to a person who may not possess an official position within the organization, yet has earned followers trust and respect through action— whether good or bad.

For example, an athlete on a sports team may gain *informal authority* when she scores the winning point in the final tournament. Conversely, a recently initiated gang member may gain *informal authority* for killing a rival gang leader. Although these definitions may seem clear on paper, the lines of demarcation are not always so distinct when operationalized. To better understand authority, we must also understand the nature of *roles*.

Role

Some social scientists analyze groups by examining how power is bestowed upon individual members. They observe that some power is *positional,* in other words it comes with the job title: When you have the title, or role, you have the power. A corporation's CEO, the Chief of Police or an Army General will have a certain amount of power given to them by the nature of their position within their organizations. For our purposes, we will call this a *formal authority role*.

In contrast to position power is *personal* power. This is the power, or authority, one earns through one's reputation and is influenced by one's leadership, character and actions, among many other factors. For our purposes, we will call this an *informal authority role*. How one gains informal authority is a complex yet fascinating group dynamics process.

Let us consider the 1986 Vietnam War movie *Platoon*[33] and the group of soldiers represented within it. As the senior officer in his platoon, Lieutenant Wolfe holds a *formal authority role* and, as a result, all orders from above are issued through him. But the inexperienced Wolfe clearly garners little respect—and therefore little trust and power—from the war weary soldiers supposedly in his charge. Instead, the soldiers are divided in their *informal authorization* of two Sergeants: Sergeant "Elias" Grodin and Staff Sergeant Bob "Barnes," who both elicit power and trust from their loyal followers based on their strong characters and war fighting acumen.

Although Wolfe is designated as the *formal authority*, authorized to perform certain services on behalf of the squad, he provides little actual leadership to the platoon. Instead, when it comes to important tactical decisions, the soldiers dismiss Wolfe's inputs and follow their *informal authorities:* Elias and Barnes. As a result, two types of authority roles emerge: a weak *formal authority role*, represented by Wolfe, and strong *informal authority roles*, represented by Elias and Barnes.

How Groups Award *Informal Authority Roles*

To understand how groups award informal authority, we continue with our analysis of the movie *Platoon*. We see that each soldier in the unit takes up a number of different *roles* within the group over time. For example, Staff Sergeant Barnes, referred to as "Captain Ahab",[34] is at times fortune teller, tactical leader, tough-love motivator, and disciplinarian. Some soldiers in the platoon believe Barnes to be a hero, others believe him to be the devil, as the lines between good and evil become blurred under the stress of combat.

Similarly, Sergeant Elias occupies a number of different roles depending on whose perspective is being represented. Sometimes seen as a concerned, intuitive team player, Elias often leads by example, taking on the most dangerous assignments. Yet, Elias is also seen by some as a self-involved social crusader, a "water walker" only interested in furthering his own social agenda, a pothead who escapes reality through drugs.

While Barnes often represents the dark side of human instinct to ravage and destroy, Elias represents the need for kindness, justice and hope for the future, even in the most stressful and chaotic situations. These descriptors could also be considered *informal authority roles*. But how do these roles get assigned?

Barnes and Elias are used by the platoon as repositories for feelings that are uncomfortable, too difficult for the group to cope with. Feelings such as fear of death, injury, failure or cowardice. The soldiers disown these unpleasant feelings and their responsibility to act, by investing their hope and support in the leadership of these two men. As a result, ***Barnes and Elias represent both informal and formal authority roles*** at different times.

For example, both men have gained a strong following among certain subgroups within the platoon. Through their actions they gained *informal authority*—power and trust—from their troops. Yet, as senior enlisted men they are also in *formal authority roles*. In other words, they are charged with certain responsibilities and from that charge have a certain positional power over their men. Note, for instance, Sergeant Barnes' behavior when he believes that the young new Private, Chris Taylor, has turned against him; he assigns Taylor all sorts of arduous activities like digging fox holes and cleaning latrines, assignments well within Barnes' jurisdiction from his *formal authority role*. Taylor complies, respecting Barnes' *formal authority* as his platoon Sergeant, yet he backs Elias' *informal authority* awarding him much more trust and power than he does Barnes.

During a dangerous nighttime patrol near the Cambodian border the team's internal conflicts finally split the platoon, one side aligning behind Barnes, the other behind Elias. As the story continues, we see that Taylor has mobilized support for Elias from his own *informal authority role*. In other words although Taylor, the most junior man in the platoon, does not have *formal* authority, he still garners a strong, subtle influence over his fellow soldiers. Through his self-sacrifice, hard work and honest character,

Taylor begins to have an impact on his fellow soldiers, gaining *informal* authority as he builds power and trust.

Why Is It Important To Understand *Roles*?

It is important to understand the difference between *formal authority roles*, or position power, and *informal authority roles*, or personal power, because of the complex psychological dynamics that occur during the group's act of authorization. In other words, does a group completely give over its power and responsibility to the formal authority CEO in order to act like dependent, blameless victims when things go wrong? Or do they retain their autonomy as thinking professionals, able to exercise their informal authority by taking responsibility for awarding trust and power, as they authorize that CEO to act?

The process by which crowds, groups and teams award authority can be quite complex and research has shown that the individual with the best leadership skills does not always emerge. For instance, sometimes called the *babble effect,* one predictor of who a group selects as its leader is how frequently the individual speaks regardless of what they actually say.[35] Apparently quantity not quality of communication is viewed by some as a positive indication of leadership skills.

In other studies it was found that leaders often tend to be taller, older and have more physical abilities than their followers, even though these characteristics usually have little relationship to leadership skills. Although gender does not correlate to leader effectiveness, men are still five times more likely than women to be group leaders.[36] How do these seemingly arbitrary characteristics get assigned as positive leadership characteristics? To more fully understand these dynamics, it is important to examine how participation in crowds, groups and teams stirs up anxiety in most people.

Joining Anxiety

Participating in crowds, groups and teams often causes anxiety in individuals who feel conflicted about 'joining.' Most people want to belong and enjoy the camaraderie and safety of being part of something. At the same time, they may feel reluctant to commit and threatened about their loss of individual identity. This often results in two distinct, yet competing feelings: Fear of being swallowed up, or fused, by the power of the group and fear of rejection and abandonment.

While the nature of this "*fusion-abandonment* tension may not be self-evident to the individual in the group setting, the anxiety that emanates from it usually is."[37] This anxiety is the result of a number of sensations occurring simultaneously within the group; Feelings such as excitement about the future, potentialities of group membership, making new friends, engaging in interesting experiences and expanding one's horizons. Yet, people may also feel uncertain about fitting in, fearful of being seen as less competent, or distracted by memories of past bad group experiences.

"When such anxiety is stirred, the individual usually becomes preoccupied by a secondary fear, that this anxiety may escalate" and the group may "get out of hand."[38] Therefore, groups initially attempt to keep things 'under control' by ignoring their anxiety, pretending it does not exist, and engaging in behaviors that seem acceptable to most group members. As a result two strategies often emerge: One approach is to remain connected and undifferentiated as a group, operating under the assumption that everyone agrees on everything that is being said and done; the second approach involves holding back, employing a wait-and-see attitude as things evolve.

Unfortunately each of these approaches stirs up more anxiety, fueling the group's *fusion-abandonment* concerns. In an attempt to ease its growing anxiety, the group may now try the opposite strategy. For instance, once vocal members may now be ignored by the group while the less interactive may now be moved to the forefront. In either scenario the group often acts as if only the self assigned task—whatever task it is—could be accomplished, all will be saved. As it becomes clear that the measures employed to alleviate the tensions are not working, and group anxiety is actually escalating, the group begins to feel like a very unsafe place.

The group is now confronted with a *paradox*: It may be personally dangerous to invest energy in this process, but if one does not jump in and gain some influence, things may spiral out of control. In either case, life within this group begins to feel quite risky. This switch—from managing self-processes to making judgments about the group-as-a-whole—especially as individual anxiety is increasing, is a difficult yet significant human process often represented in both psychological and anthropological literature as *splitting*.[39]

Splitting

Initially introduce by psychoanalyst Melanie Klein (see chapter five), the concept of *splitting* has gained wider popularity and use outside of psychoanalysis in recent years. The Oxford American dictionary describes *splitting* as the act of breaking into parts and this definition is congruent with Klein's use of the term.

Klein observed that when anxiety becomes high, people have a tendency to manage their discomfort by dividing, or *splitting*, their feelings and *projecting* or attaching these feelings on all-good and all-bad *objects*. In this manner, someone or something else is made to take on the all-bad characteristics that the individual unconsciously wants to disown, allowing the individual to retain the all-good feeling for themselves. By *projecting* these disowned all-bad parts onto another, the individual attempts to alleviate their anxiety.

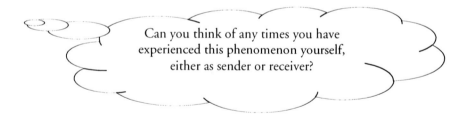

Can you think of any times you have experienced this phenomenon yourself, either as sender or receiver?

Other theorists, such as Wilfred Bion, applied Klein's theories observing that groups behave in a very similar manner to individuals (see chapter three and five for more about Bion). One of the key consequences of *splitting* in organizations is that certain subgroups are expected to carry unpleasant emotions for the entire system. For example, in *Platoon*, the conflict between Barnes and Elias represents this all-bad, all-good dichotomy. To some soldiers, Barnes was the hero and Elias the traitor, to others Barnes was the devil and Elias the savior.

Here is another example: Have you ever been part of an organization that had *one* troubled department? It was common knowledge throughout the organization that if only that *one* department could get themselves organized, things would finally run smoothly. Fantasizing that this *one* department was all-bad allowed the rest of the organization to feel all-good about their own performance. Yet, no matter who worked in that department, it remained the *scapegoat* for the entire system. No one could ever fix it. The problem with this organization was that certain 'unwanted' or 'difficult' feelings—such as competition, envy and fear of failure—were not being dealt with directly within the organization. Instead, these uncomfortable feelings were *split off* and *projected* onto the one problem department, as if that was where the issue lay, when in fact, the problem existed throughout the organization.

Interestingly, just like in *Platoon*, those individuals and subgroups "being projected upon are usually doing their own fair share of splitting and projection" [40] as well. In other words, subgroups may mutually cooperate in relocating their hatred in the other, or *scapegoating*, so they can feel good about themselves and their group as a result. Much of this occurs below the surface. So subtly, unconsciously, and routinely that it is difficult to notice. In fact, because it becomes part of the organization's culture, challenging it feels a little like disloyalty to the organization itself. Can you think of other examples you have observed of this process?

The *Scapegoat*

The term *scapegoat* originates in an ancient Jewish custom during which a goat was released into the wilderness after religious leaders had symbolically laid the sins of the people upon it. Therefore, a *scapegoat* is a person or group who undeservedly is made to bear the blame or punishment for others.

Scapegoating occurs often in groups. As the group struggles to mange its anxiety, it may construct a fictitious *group-in-the mind* where everyone agrees and conforms to the emerging norms. As long as each group member pretends that they are in fact 'just like everyone else,' the group can enjoy this idealized identity and share a spirit of a spirit of cohesion and love, feeling proud to be included.

Yet, this group is founded on an idealized world created through blind faith, a world that only exists because people believe in it. In fact, no two people are alike. Depending on what the characteristics of the 'in-group' are, demographic factors such as race, gender, sexual orientation, religion, age, height, weight, attractiveness, family connections, friendships and others can all come into play as the group awards *informal authority*.

Although it may make people feel good to 'pretend' to be included, the negative side of this type of thinking creates *scapegoating*, patterns of exclusion and intolerance of difference.[41] People who question or do not conform to the group's fantasy of perfection are attacked and excluded. As a result, there is a strong pull toward conformity and **groupthink**.

Groupthink

Groupthink is a model developed by sociologist Irving Janis to show how group decisionmaking can go wrong. "Groupthink is a drive for consensus at the cost of realistic consideration of alternative ideas."[42] It occurs when group members suppress their personal ideas, putting social acceptance and group harmony above reaching a good decision.[43] But why would smart people do such a thing?

First, the suppression of ideas is not always deliberate or conscious. People voluntarily comply because they are affected by the power of group processes. Second, *groupthink* members often believe their group to be invulnerable and beyond reproach. As long as members have faith, the group feels confident things will work out. Third, because the group is operating under the illusion of invulnerability, they simply cannot see contradictory evidence. They can only see the data that supports their decision, not data that confounds it. Finally, similar to **splitting** described previously, *groupthink* members foster a competitive, 'us and them' climate, stereotyping outsiders and challengers as the 'enemy.' As a result, the group maintains themselves as all-good and labels their competitors as all-bad. Any one who voices dissent is either ignored or forced out of the group to join the all-bad outsiders.

Space Shuttle Challenger: *Groupthink?*

Let us consider events leading up to the explosion of the Space Shuttle *Challenger* on January 28, 1986 as an example of *groupthink*. After decades of success in space exploration, NASA found itself in the 1980s under pressure to keep up its ambitious project schedule, yet remain within tight budgetary constraints. Pushed to do more with fewer resources, a new organizational climate emerged.

As Senator John Glenn put it, in the early days at NASA when he was an Astronaut, there "was a can-do attitude" yet "safety was paramount." Overtime, he noted, the "can-do attitude" was "replaced by a can't fail attitude,"[44] which permeated the organization. Deluded by its history of success, NASA acted as if it was infallible, launching the shuttle despite several urgent warnings by mid- and lower-level employees about the deterioration of O-ring seals. The shuttle might "blow-up" NASA directors were informed. Yet, rather than delay the launch to investigate these warnings, NASA charged ahead as the concerns were submerged by a 'macho' organizational culture of 'we can do anything.'[45] The *Challenger* exploded on launch, killing all seven of its crew members.

Why was this accident not prevented? NASA had succumbed to *groupthink* as an invulnerable attitude developed, blinding directors to the evidence that the shuttle was not safe to launch. Employees attempting to voice concern were either ignored or forced out, as a competitive 'us-and-them' culture emerged. In the end, rational decisionmaking and safety were sacrificed in favor of social acceptance and group harmony.

Summary

After reading this chapter, you should have a better understanding of some key terms we will be using throughout this program. Terms such as:

- *Crowds, groups* and *teams*
- *Leadership* and *management*
- *Authority* and the *act of authorizing*

- *Formal* and *informal* authority roles
- *Scapegoating, groupthink* and other group dynamics phenomenon.

Now it is time to become familiar with some more ideas about leadership and their application to high-risk teams and organizations today.

——————▼——————

CHAPTER III

DYNAMICS OF LEADERSHIP IN GROUPS: SOME BASIC THEORIES

LEARNING OBJECTIVES

1. Compare different theories of leadership in groups.
2. Distinguish between technical and adaptive challenges in high-risk teams.
3. Outline some questions to consider when evaluating leadership and the health of a team or organization.

Introduction

In the previous chapter, we discussed some important definitions to consider when analyzing group dynamics in high-risk teams. This chapter continues the dialogue, exploring the contributions of various experts in the field of leadership and group theory reviewing questions to consider when evaluating leadership and the health of a team or organization. First, we examine *organizations* and how they use teams.

Most social scientists agree that *organizations*, as we understand them today in the Western world, are a relatively recent phenomenon, only emerging over the past 150 years. Although there are some longstanding examples from history such as the army, church or government dating back thousands of years, organizations, as we think about them, are much more recent. As the concept of the *organization* emerged over time, our identities became inextricably linked to the organizations we interacted with such as where we work, went to school, go for leisure activities or shop. In this way, our society has empowered organizations to take on a life of their own, influencing the way we think about them and ourselves.[46] As a result organizations remain "puzzling terrain because they lend themselves to multiple, conflicting interpretations, all of which are plausible."[47] Whose interpretations carry more *authority* is an interesting question.

Much of the work that goes on within organizations, especially in high-risk professions, takes place in teams, squads and crews. Therefore, an organization can essentially be thought of as a **group of teams**, fostering similar dynamics as those previously described in chapter two. For example, organizational life can cause anxiety as questions about competency, feeling valued and belonging, and can be offset by fear of being swamped or losing individuality and control. Squads and crews can scapegoat each other, fueled by intergroup rivalry and competition.

As relationships develop within the high-risk team, the moods of others—actual or perceived—can have an exaggerated impact on members' thinking as the ***fusion-abandonment*** dynamic discussed in chapter two appears. Some team members may become hyper-sensitive to feelings of loyalty, anger, anxiety and fear especially with regard to *authority* figures. Not necessarily negative, these powerful unconscious forces can be harnessed for both productivity as well as destruction depending on the success of leadership efforts. Several scholars have offered their insights into these interesting organizational dynamics as a way to evaluate leadership efforts.

Oscillations of Organizational Life

Leadership scholars have offered several ways to consider leadership within groups, teams and organizations over the years. For example, Tavistock psychoanalyst and decorated British World War I and II veteran Wilfred Bion observed that groups oscillate between a state of productive work, which he termed the *Work group* and a number of possible defensive positions called *basic assumptions.*

Bion hypothesized that the *Work group* focuses intently on the group's task and maintains close contact with reality, resisting group dynamics such as *splitting* and *groupthink* described in chapter two. Conversely, the *basic assumptions* group's primary task is to ease the group's anxieties and avoid the pain or emotions that further work might bring. When operating in this mode, the group '*acts as if*' certain dynamics were indisputable facts, evident for all to see.

Bion identified three basic types of *basic assumption* modes: *dependence, pairing,* and *fight-flight.*[48] When a group operates in the *dependency* mode, Bion noted:

> One person is always felt to be in a position to supply the needs of the group, and the rest in a position to which their needs are supplied…having thrown all their cares on the leader, they sit back and wait for him to solve all their problems…the dependent group soon shows that an integral part of its structure is a belief in the omniscience and omnipotence of some one member of the group.[49]

The group '*acts as if*' this *leader*, whether selected formally or informally, has clairvoyance of thought and supernatural powers and that the rest of the group is powerless and dependent. When the leader fails to meet the group's unrealistic expectations, as he or she inevitably does, the group becomes quickly frustrated and disappointedly *selects* another member for the daunting task. This leader will also fail eventually, of course.[50]

The **basic assumption mode of** *pairing* is evident in a group when it invests irrational hopefulness for the future in two of the group members.

Regardless of gender, the group *'acts as if'* these two individuals have paired either for a metaphoric *sexual* experience, which would provide the birth of a new group, a religious experience, which would provide a messiah, or a *reparative* experience, which would produce world peace.

When a group operates in the **basic assumption mode of** *fight-flight*, Bion wrote:

> The group seems to know only two techniques of self-preservation, fight or flight…the kind of leadership that is recognized as appropriate is the leadership of the man who mobilizes the group to attack somebody, or alternatively to lead it in flight…leaders who neither fight nor run away are not easily understood.[51]

As described, Bion noted that when fears and emotions arise in a group, the group swings away from *Work* mode toward a *basic assumption mode* in an effort to address and contain the group's anxiety. Yet, he reminded us optimistically that "one of the striking things about a group is that, despite the influence of the basic assumptions, it is the *W group* that triumphs in the long run."[52] In other words although groups and teams evoke a series of mixed emotions and anxieties from their members, productivity eventually prevails.

Bion's theories can be particularly helpful when considering analyzing high-risk teams because of the intense nature of these team's operating environments. It is often joked among pilots and police officers that their jobs consist of 'hours of endless boredom broken up by moments of sheer terror.' The nature of this intense, action oriented environment lends itself to Bion's basic assumptions. In order to understand how we might apply Bion's theories in this situation, let us review the contributions of another early Tavistock scholar, Pierre Turquet.

Dynamics of the 'Work Group'

Turquet hypothesized that one can identify Bion's sophisticated *Work group* by observing a team's use of: *1) leadership, 2) the skills of its mem-*

bers, 3) testable hypotheses, and 3) relevant basic assumptions in support of its work. Therefore, the commercial aviation industry seeks to mobilize *dependency* in order to have well-behaved passengers and the military seeks to mobilize the *fight* side of *fight-flight* to have courageous soldiers.

First, the successful high-risk team will share the leadership role, allowing the most skilled member of the group to emerge as leader. In this manner, the team is not dominated by one forceful, authoritarian individual but *shares the leadership role* depending on the team's shifting primary task.

Second, to facilitate this, the team "seeks in a sophisticated way to protect the skills of its individual members."[53] For example, group members exercise a sense of personal responsibility, managing themselves and their anxieties rather than loading up the leader to take care of them. If members are unable to tolerate their own anxiety, "efforts are often made to deskill the leader by various members of the group, who fill him up with their anxieties and fantasies"[54] and the group will swing into a defensive or *basic assumption* mode.

Third, a successful high-risk team is curious about its own behavior and will use testable hypotheses based on a predictive "because" clause to further their work rather than rumors and unreliable hunches. For instance, the team might ponder: It seems that members of this team are not committed to the task *because* few members show up on time and are not prepared to discuss the stated agenda. Now that the team has identified, named and therefore *surfaced a conflict*, it can then attempt to find a viable solution.

Fourth, the successful high-risk team seeks to make a sophisticated use of the relevant *basic assumption* group for the implementation of its primary task.[55] In this way, the team might effectively use fight-flight mode as a way to motivate soldiers to protect their squad or athletes to compete more intensely.[56] By analyzing these four factors, one can evaluate the effectiveness of leadership efforts in high-risk teams and organizations. Other scholars made significant contributions in this area as well.

Socio-Technical Dimensions of Work Systems

In the 1940s, 1950s, and 1960s, studies in coal mines, textile mills, and hospitals conducted by Tavistock members Elliott Jaques, A. K. Rice, Eric Miller, Eric Trist, Harold Bridger, and Isabel Menzies, among others, all proved influential to the development of another important organizational concept, the *socio-technical* perspective. Analyzing work as a *socio-technical* system provided a way to optimize both human elements and technological imperatives within organizations, without sacrificing one to the other. Yet, the *socio-technical* system approach focused at the level of what Bion would have termed the primary work group rather than the wider organization and its environment.

Further developments in *open system theory* by Miller and Rice[57] made it possible to look simultaneously at the relationships between the individual worker and the work group, the work group and the organization, and the organization and its environment. In other words, *open systems* theory built upon, yet expanded, the premise of the *socio-technical* system in ways that permitted an understanding of the operation of the organization's internal dynamics as well as its interaction with its external environment.

As Rice described it, the classic model of an organization is one of a *closed system,* a mechanically self sufficient organization neither importing nor exporting across the boundaries of the organization. Rice noted, "*Open systems,* in contrast, exist and can only exist by the exchange of materials with their environment…the process of importing, converting, and exporting materials is the work the system has to do to live."[58] Miller provided examples to illustrate Rice's point:

> Thus a manufacturing company coverts raw materials into saleable products (and waste), a college converts freshmen into graduates (and drop-outs) and there are the other resources that are required to bring about the processing: the production workers, the teachers, the machinery, the supplies, etc. The boundary across which these materials flow in and out both separates the enterprise from and links it with its environment.[59]

Boundaries

Since *open system* theorists were particularly concerned with how teams and organizations import and export, the permeability of the *boundary* region came to be viewed as a critical area for the *exercise of leadership*. For example, if leadership is lax and the boundary becomes too porous, it is possible that the outside environment can become too influential and disruptive to the internal work of the team or organization. Conversely, if the leadership and boundary is too rigid the internal organization can stagnate and become inflexible to market or environmental changes. Therefore, Miller noted, "survival is therefore contingent on an appropriate degree of insulation and permeability in the boundary region."[60] The idea of *boundary management* has been applied to thinking about an individual's as well as an organization's boundary.

Although they were both anthropologists and business consultants, Miller[61] and Rice[62] incorporated psychological theories into their thinking about groups and organizations, in particular, the concepts of *splitting* and *projection* discussed in chapter two. For instance, Rice described how "in the mature individual, the ego—the concept of the self as a unique individual—mediates the relationships between the internal world of good and bad objects and the external world of reality, and thus takes, in relations to the personality, a 'leadership' role." [63]

Therefore, when one is involved in organizational life, one is influenced both by the external environment of the work setting, as well as by one's own internal environment, which is largely a product of previous work and childhood experiences. In Rice's words, "The mature ego is one that can define the boundary between what is inside and what is outside, and can control the transactions between the one and the other."[64] However, the group can also evoke more primitive feelings in the individual, such as those "in the areas of dependency aggression and hope. The individual is usually unaware of this process: these basic emotions slip under the guard, as it were, of his ego function."[65]

Yet, even though these primitive feelings and defenses might go undetected by the individual, they can have an impact on the group and be sensed by others within the organization.[66] When people come together in groups, individuals' primitive feelings and defenses can get mobilized on behalf of, and in service to, the group and the bad feelings are often the *split* off and *projected* onto authority figures, whose task it is to regulate the boundary region. As one method to study people's struggles with these types of authority issues, the Tavistock Institute developed the **group relations conference** in the late 1950s. The *'conference'* created an experiential learning method that linked psychoanalytic theory with the notion of *open systems* theory developed in the social sciences. We will discuss its organization and operation in chapter seven.

Task

In addition to the development of the *group relations conference*, a second result of the amalgamation of *open systems* theory with psychoanalytic theory was an expanded definition of Bion's notion of a group's *task*. As discussed previously, Bion postulated that a group operates at two levels: the sophisticated *Work group* level, which is oriented towards overt task completion, and the *basic assumption* level which sometimes supports, but more often hinders, the overt task by acting defensively.[67]

Rice used *open systems* and its theories about the importance of boundary management to re-conceptualize the notion of task, calling the task that a group "must perform if it is to survive" the group's *primary task*.[68] Although all organizations must perform a complex set of tasks on a daily basis, in most cases, he argued, one task was the most critical one. An organization must perform this *primary task* to continue to be the organization it claimed to be. Rice argued that environmental constraints such as political, economic, legal, and social contexts within which an organization operates further influence an organization's primary task.[69]

An example of how an organization's primary task can shift in an open system due to environmental changes can be found in the days and months following the terrorist attacks in the United States on September 11, 2001. Whether an organization's primary task had been educating children, flying commercial airliners, or winning football games in the National Football League, organizational priorities shifted in response to these environmental changes. Many organizations made safety and secu-

rity their new *primary task*, at least temporarily, adjusting policies and procedures accordingly.

Assessing Leadership

More recently, American organizational consultant Lawrence
Hirshhorn[70] contributed further to understanding the organizational
health and repercussions of leadership efforts in group and organizations.
He noted four indicators of healthy leadership in organizations:

First, assess the amount of time people spend doing *real work* where
individual's talents, efforts and productivity are allowed to shine, versus
time dedicated to *organizational processes* such as internal memo writing,
preparing for meetings and satisfying unwarranted levels of perfection.

Second, assess whether resources and promotions are awarded based on
merit or on personal relationships. Third, assess whether leaders protect followers from excessive worry by containing worker's anxieties about the
future with their vision, thereby allowing them to focus on their work. Or, in
contrast, do followers protect leaders by withholding information in an
effort to be loyal and make their boss look good. Fourth, assess the extent to
which individuals feel linked together through concerted actions as a group
with a common task.[71] By analyzing these four important factors, one can
understand better the effectiveness of leadership efforts.

Indicators of Successful Leadership

Other ways to evaluate leadership efforts in teams and organizations
have been offered by Harvard professor Ronald A. Heifetz and organizational consultant Donald L. Laurie. They propose that a successful leader
attends to three fundamental tasks in order to motivate followers: 1)
**Create a positive work environment; 2) Manage rate of change; and 3)
Communicate confidence.**[72]

First, a leader must create a "holding environment," regulating tension
by turning up the organizational heat or venting off steam, as required by
the situation. To accomplish this leaders must "get to the balcony" to
observe the larger organizational picture. Second, a leader is responsible for

managing the rate of change, providing "direction, protection, orientation, managing conflict and sharpening norms."[73] Since people frequently avoid things that disturb them, a leader's job is to get people to confront tough situations and surface conflict in order to use it as a source of creativity. Third, a leader must communicate confidence with their presence and poise. He or she must be able to tolerate frustration, uncertainty and pain without getting overly anxious, in order to hold steady and maintain organizational tension.

In addition to these three factors, Heifetz and Laurie propose that some leadership challenges have prescribed *technical* solutions—steps dictated by manuals, procedures or checklists—to solve certain problems. Yet, many of an organization's most demanding challenges are often ambiguous problems with no clear solutions, called *adaptive* challenges. These problems require innovative and creative leadership to solve.

Yet in many fields, especially high-risk industries, people are trained to take action following prescribed solutions in technical manuals and checklists. Even when pausing to reflect would be prudent, it is difficult for high-risk teams to break their action-oriented mindset. Although information may be limited, high-risk teams may find it difficult to *tolerate ambiguity* and wait for vital information to become available to assist in decision making. Heifetz and Laurie offer some strategies for leaders to employ when confronted with these challenges:

> ➢ "Get to the balcony" in order to observe the bigger picture.

> ➢ Separate the technical, prescribed challenges from the adaptive, ambiguous ones.

> ➢ Create the holding environment by managing the speed of change.

> ➢ Get conflict out in the open.

> ➢ Give work back to the people by authorizing at the lowest possible level.

> ➢ Protect voices from outside, the original thinkers, whistleblowers, and creative deviants who are not afraid to speak the truth.[74]

Other Thoughts about Evaluating Leadership

Although this chapter outlined the nature of leadership within high-risk teams and organizational life, offering some ways to think about evaluation, it was not meant to be exhaustive or to infer leadership is a formulaic process. The purpose of this discussion was intended to familiarize the reader with *some* of the discussions on the topic of leadership in order to stimulate thought and instill a sense of curiosity about the nature of leadership in the many areas of our lives. I would like to offer a few more concluding thoughts about evaluating leadership efforts.

After observing teams and organizations, one phenomenon I have written about is how the innovation and creativity required to energize work and keep an organization relevant ironically can become the focus of attacks and inter-group rivalries, creating a cycle that puts the organization itself at risk.[75] Partly this results from the fact that although innovation and collaboration are required in today's fast paced environment, people become personally attached to and invested in their ideas. In fact, individuals can feel so closely identified with 'their' ideas that it becomes difficult to separate their ideas from themselves: *my idea is me, I am my idea*. Strong emotional bonds connecting people with their ideas intensify conflicts that inevitably develop between groups advocating one approach or another to an organization's work. Consequently, if an idea is rejected—or we might say when an idea is rejected, because organizations must constantly innovate—this rejection can be experienced as a personal attack. *You reject my idea; you reject me.*

One way to observe these dynamics at work is by considering how organizational restructuring often can be played out as if it were an inter-generational family drama. The older generation often experiences their once popular theories and methods coming under attack, even being deemed obsolete. This group experiences the necessary reorganization as a personal attack, as if not only their ideas but they themselves are being discarded. Conversely, the younger generation may feel personally slighted, that without periodic restructuring their innovations cannot flourish, their full capacities remain unrecognized and they can never 'grow-up' and be accepted as full members of the organization. They feel as if they have inherited the family business, but have been asked simply to maintain what the older generation originated.

As a result of these conflicts about change, organizational tensions can alienate members, in this case the 'young' from the 'old,' both of whom feel unappreciated, causing feuds and splits to develop and making once productive participants feel estranged and unable to work. Disenfranchised workers often can be heard to say things like "we tried that eight years ago and it didn't work then," "so and so tried that, see where it got him," and other statements reflecting each group's struggle to keep pace with the change. If allowed to develop in the extreme, such feuds and splits can lead to disastrous intra-organizational rivalries, where talented people, unable or unwilling to adjust to organizational change or uncomfortable with the tensions, drift away at tremendous cost to the organization's productivity. In the end, people wonder whether they are living through an organizational transformation or witnessing a slow organizational death. Can you think of some examples of this in your organizations?

In order to mitigate destructive rivalries and conflicts, and maximize positive change, I contend that organizations must expect to evolve their theories and methodologies, and restructure their institutions at least once every ten years. Such *restructuring must be expected, if not demanded*, so that organizations can continue to thrive. Without periodic revision, organizations risk losing vitality and relevance, slipping into obscurity like last year's fashion.

When considering the overall health of an organization, I also suggest one examine a few additional key areas. First, assess how diversity and the role of 'the other' have been represented within the organization. For instance, is it difficult for women, people of color, gays or the 'new guy' to be fully present within the organization? Is diversity actively embraced as a benefit to the entire organization or is it something merely tolerated, requiring 'the other' to modify their behavior to fit in?

Second, assess how conflict is handled within the organization. Is it allowed to surface and be dispelled or is it forced underground to resurface in other areas? Third, assess where the 'real work' gets accomplished. Is it done in formal workspaces such as meetings or informal places like the restroom or golf course? Fourth, assess how rigid the organization's hierarchy is. If an employee does not get satisfaction, can he or she seek assistance above his supervisor without fear of retribution? Fifth, assess whether an individual's skills are used effectively or squandered on meaningless tasks better suited for someone else. Sixth, assess whether employees are mentored to continue to grow or stifled into submission.

Looking for evidence of these items can help to determine the effectiveness of leadership and the overall health of a team or organization. Think about your own experiences of organizational life. Can you add any more to the list?

CHAPTER IV

▼

'CREW' RESOURCE MANAGEMENT

LEARNING OBJECTIVES

1. Clarify the definition of *Crew Resource Management (CRM)*.
2. Explain how individual measures of performance became standardized within the airline industry, as an example of the dynamics common in many high-risk organizations.
3. Explain how *authority* influences high-risk teams' performance.
4. Describe the *four skill areas* new team training models should address for high-risk teams.

Introduction

Given the complexity of leadership and team dynamics, is it possible to increase people's awareness in order to perform more effectively in high-risk teams? I believe it is. The previous chapters outlined important foundational information, building our knowledge and awareness of factors influencing performance in high-risk teams. Now that we understand some key terms and definitions, we can apply these tools to analyze existing team training models.

Although numerous team training models exist, exploring how professionals in high-risk fields might increase their awareness of: 1) **The dynamics of authority relations; 2) factors affecting the** *act of authorizing*; **and 3) the interdependent nature of leadership, while 4) assisting participants to learn how to manage anxiety and continue to think and function in stressful situations** has not been undertaken until recently. In the following sections we examine the history, theories and methods of some existing team training models.

One of the first high-risk team training models developed is called *Crew Resource Management (CRM)*. We begin our review with a brief history of the evolution of CRM and its roots in *individualistic* measures of job performance—as compared to more modern notions exploring a team's performance. Developed in the 1980s in the field of aviation, CRM has proven popular over the years, spreading to other technical fields. Both its success and its limitations warrant further examination.

Crew Resource Management (CRM) Defined

Defined as the use of "all available resources—information, equipment, and people—to achieve safe and efficient flight operations,"[76] CRM is more than just a training practice. **CRM is considered to be an organizational philosophy utilizing teamwork and open communication to manage errors in high-risk teams.**[77]

Initially termed *Cockpit* Resource Management, CRM emerged largely as a bi-product of the Jet Age, morphing into *Crew* Resource Management when flight attendants, dispatchers and aircraft mechanics joined pilots in the training. As jet aircraft became the mainstay of commercial air travel in the 1960s, the safety and reliability of jet engines drastically reduced both maintenance problems and the number of aviation accidents, illuminating the fact that **human errors played a part in 70-80% of aircraft mishaps.** "The conclusion drawn from these investigations was that 'pilot error' in documented accidents and incidents was more likely to reflect failures in team communication and coordination than deficiencies in 'stick-and-rudder' proficiency."[78]

In other words, misunderstandings and miscommunication between crew inside the aircraft, often compounded by those with others outside the cockpit, were a factor in *nearly all aircraft accidents*. Yet, effecting cultural change would prove daunting as aviation's roots in individual measurements of performance proved firmly embedded.

Entrenched Ethos: Individual Proficiency

Perhaps influenced by the bravado of war fighting and barnstorming in the early twentieth-century, aviation culture historically has celebrated the courageous young dare-devil pilot and his individual flying acumen; rarely, if ever, has it lauded teamwork. Pilot training, whether conducted in military, commercial or general aviation, often was accomplished one-on-one in boot camp fashion, where flight instructors demonstrated and students unquestioningly mimicked behavior and technical maneuvers under a barrage of verbal direction. There were few standardized methods of instruction and "communication between the instructor and student was woefully inadequate, consisting mostly of shouting above the wind and engine noise."[79] The goal—and first major achievement in any pilot's career—was to *fly solo*.

Even at major commercial airlines, until very recently, a pilot was deemed competent when he or she could demonstrate proficiency flying a standard set of maneuvers. Although pilots usually fly in crews, competence had little to do with teamwork or error management in the cockpit. It is "only within the last decade" that we have "begun to consider this issue of crews and groups…in the training of teams that fly commercial aircraft."[80]

The vast majority of airline pilots have been military trained. In addition, in the US, most of the Federal Aviation Administration (FAA) inspectors who, in coordination with airline leaders, developed the training, checking, and standard operating practices were also from a military background. A homogenous group, these ex-military pilots created a culture to which they were accustomed. This culture respected rank and hierarchical *authority*, valuing captains who took charge and acted decisively and subordinates who followed orders, rarely questioning *authority* or the decisions of superiors.

Reflecting these values, industry leaders developed a training environment that measured "individual proficiency" by requiring "each captain to demonstrate the ability to handle" without assistance "nearly every conceivable situation that might be encountered in flight."[81] Called *first officers*, copilots' individual proficiency was measured by how well they assisted the captain. In fact, "in 1952 the guidelines for proficiency checks at one major airline categorically stated that the *first officer should not correct errors made by the captain*."[82]

The aviation industry is not alone in encouraging hierarchical, *authority* relationships and *individual* measurements of success. From military and law enforcement to surgery and nuclear power, most technical high-risk fields have a similar ethos entrenched. Although collaboration and teams are more prevalent than ever in a wide array of technical industries, measures of proficiency and success continue to be predominantly centered on the individual. The individualistic norms underpinning these cultures continue to reflect this early acculturation process despite the fact that the history of accidents suggests that error management depends on recognizing how *authority* relations can interfere with team performance and decisionmaking, especially under the stressful conditions high-risk teams encounter on a routine basis.

Understanding how best to operate in a team while under stress in these high-risk professions is the way of the future. The following three case studies from the field of aviation offer us a chance to examine some glaring examples of how *authority* patterns can interfere with team performance.

As you read the Florida Everglades example discussed in the next section, consider:

> ➤ If Air Traffic Controllers (ATC) had inquired with more *authority* about Eastern Airlines Flight 401's departure from its assigned altitude, could this accident have been prevented?

> ➤ If the Captain had exercised leadership more assertively, speaking with more authority, and his crew followed his directions more

attentively, would this team have fixated so completely on a "59-cent" light bulb?

A Case Study: Florida Everglades

In 1972 an aviation accident attracted the attention of aviation leaders, illuminating deficiencies in team training practices industry wide. Eastern Airlines Flight 401, a Lockheed L-1011, crashed in the Florida Everglades fatally injuring ninety-nine passengers and five crewmembers after an experienced aircrew became distracted by a burnt out landing gear light bulb. Unbeknownst to the crew, the airplane began a slow descent after a newly installed autopilot was inadvertently disconnected during their trouble-shooting.

Upon investigation the Safety Board found that many pilots interviewed did not fully understand the autopilot's features and "were unaware of the minor control column inputs needed to effect a change in the aircraft's attitude."[83] ATC compounded the communication and performance breakdown within the cockpit by their vague inquiry—"How's it goin' out there, Eastern?"—when they observed the aircraft had departed its assigned altitude on a steady descent to impact.

How had a highly trained, professional aircrew team in a modern, well-equipped jet crash their airplane over a "59-cent" light bulb? And why did ATC not inquire more specifically about the airplane's descent, taking up their *authority* to challenge the aircrew's violation of Federal Aviation Regulations by departing from its assigned altitude without clearance? Why had the pilots not been properly trained by their company on the new autopilot system? It became evident that individual, group and systemic factors all were involved in the accident's evolution.

By the mid-1970s many research studies, including several at the National Aeronautics and Space Administration (NASA), examined the human factors behind aviation accidents. Between 1968 and 1976, George Cooper and Maury White conducted a detailed analysis of commercial jet accidents worldwide, concluding that most incidents were correlated with "various failures of command, communication, and crew coordination."[84] Other research was even more specific, citing a need for increased awareness about the role of *management skills* in cockpit operations[85] Although these studies heightened awareness of core issues, it was an incident in the Canary Islands that further revealed the complex interrelatedness of *authority* relations and accidents, providing an industry wide impetus to develop new team training methods.

As you read the Tenerife example discussed in the next section, consider the influence of *authority*—actual and perceived—on people's behaviors. For example:

> ➤ If the KLM captain had more clearly understood the implications of his *authority*, and its potential to squelch input from his crew, could this accident have been prevented?

> ➤ If the KLM copilot had more clearly understood the influence the captain's *authority* had over him, and the responsibility he had to exercise his own authority, would he have acted on his knowledge and prevented the accident?

> ➤ If, as in the Eastern Airlines Florida Everglades example, ATC had more clearly asserted their *authority* as the controlling agency, could they have prevented this accident?

A Case Study: Tenerife

The most deadly aircraft collision in history occurred at Los Rodeos Airport, Tenerife on March 27, 1977 when KLM-Royal Dutch Airlines Flight 4805 collided with Pan American Flight 1736 killing 583 passengers and crew. Both 747s had diverted to the tiny mountainous airport due to bomb threats at their destination, Las Palmas. The weather was overcast and foggy upon arrival and steadily deteriorated as the two large jets loitered around the confines of the single runway, waiting for their destination to reopen.

As Chief Training Captain for the 747 fleet, the KLM captain was very experienced and routinely featured in company advertisements. His copilot was also an experienced pilot, but brand new to the 747. In fact, the captain had recently given him his 747 checkride.

The Spanish air traffic controllers had difficulty communicating in English and, exacerbated by the Dutch copilots' non-standard phraseology, there were numerous misunderstandings. After a lengthy delay, Las Palmas reopened and the two jumbo jets attempted to maneuver for takeoff within the limits of the small airport.

KLM taxied down the foggy runway first, turning 180-degrees into position for takeoff. Unbeknownst to the eager Dutch captain, Pan Am was taxiing immediately up the runway behind them. As the KLM Captain began the takeoff roll the copilot exclaimed "Wait a minute, we don't have an ATC clearance." The captain braked, responding "No…I know that. Go ahead and ask." Dutifully, the copilot asked for takeoff clearance and was told to "standby for takeoff."

Nevertheless, the eager KLM captain said "Let's go" and initiated his takeoff again. The copilot, clearly alarmed, exclaimed meaninglessly over the radio "we are now at takeoff!" further confusing communications between Pan Am and ATC.

The fog was so thick, neither ATC nor the taxiing Pan Am crew could see the end of the runway or KLM accelerating down it. Seconds later the Pan Am crew identified KLM's lights coming out of the fog and frantically attempted to clear the runway as the KLM captain rotated, forcing the jet into flight. Although KLM's nose gear passed over the other 747, the main landing gear sheered off Pan Am's upper deck and both aircraft were destroyed by fire.

Accident investigators determined that poor communication and use of non-standard terminology were the main causes of the collision and resultant deaths. Perhaps even more importantly, analysts wondered why such an experienced KLM crew could make such a basic, yet catastrophic, mistake. Why was the KLM captain so reluctant to accept input and why did the copilot, who clearly knew they had not been issued takeoff clearance, not speak up more assertively to prevent this accident?

In a break with aviation tradition novel for 1977, "safety analysts believed it was possible that the first officer, who had only 95 hours in the 747, and who was flying with the KLM chief 747 instructor, *may have been intimidated by the captain's legendary status.*"[86] In other words, the cause of the accident was an *authority issue*. The combination of the captain's impressive persona and the copilot's lack of confidence flying a new airplane resulted in an experienced copilot becoming confused, questioning his sense-making capabilities. Was this example of the powerful influence of *authority* dynamics over human behavior an anomaly? History proves otherwise.

As you read this third example, once again consider the influence of *authority*: An experienced and dominating Captain and two younger and less experienced crew members. For example, as in the Tenerife example:

> ➢ If the United captain had more clearly understood the implications of his *authority*, and its potential to silence any dissenting opinions in his crew, could this accident have been prevented?

> ➢ If the United copilot and flight engineer had more clearly understood the silencing influence this dominating captain's *authority* had over them, could they have spoken up and convinced him to land sooner?

A Case Study: Portland, Oregon

A third stunning breakdown in teamwork, also compounded by *authority* issues, occurred just a year and a half later when a United Airlines DC-8 ran out of fuel six miles from its destination. Although the copilot and flight engineer attempted to draw attention to the aircraft's dangerously low fuel state, the highly experienced and authoritarian captain pushed forward his agenda, paying little attention to the growing concerns of his crew.

On December 28, 1978 United Flight 173 lowered the landing gear for arrival in Portland, Oregon and the crew observed an unsafe landing gear indication followed by a loud thump, abnormal vibration and aircraft yaw. Although the backup systems indicated that the gear was in fact safely down and locked properly, the captain requested a holding pattern to communicate with company maintenance, dispatch, and destination operations about the aircraft's status.

The captain grew increasingly fixated on the chance that the gear might collapse on landing, igniting onboard fuel supplies. As a result, he delayed landing for almost an hour as he coordinated with flight attendants for a possible emergency evacuation on touchdown. The captain became so distracted by these self assigned tasks, when the copilot informed him the first of their four engines would soon fail the captain inquired "Why?" As first one engine then another dropped off due to fuel starvation, the captain finally recognized the severity of the situation demanding "You gotta keep 'em running...." and the flight engineer dutifully replied "Yes, sir."

The National Transportation Safety Board determined that the probable cause of the accident was not only the captain's failure to monitor and respond to the aircraft's low fuel state but also the failure of the first officer and flight engineer to make him aware of the severity of the situation. Although the Board recognized that "the stature of a captain and his management style may exert subtle pressure on his crew to conform to his way of thinking and may hinder interaction and adequate monitoring, forcing another crewmember to yield his right to express an opinion" they concluded that the other aircrew were also culpable exemplifying a "recurring problem"[87] industry wide.

As a result, the Safety Board recommended the development of an assertiveness training program for all airline cockpit and cabin crewmembers as part of a new standard curriculum. Fortunately, this recommendation was embraced whole heartedly by the aviation community and as a result, we have today an evolved form of *Crew Resource Management* being implemented in most commercial airlines and military squadrons worldwide, and spreading to other high-risk professions.[88]

The Emergence of Aircrew Training Programs

In less than six years, between 1972 and 1978, almost seven hundred people had been needlessly killed in aviation accidents, hundreds more seriously injured, all involving poor teamwork, aircrew error and US air carriers. Aviation industry leaders knew they desperately needed a new team training model which could address aviation's entrenched ethos and the complex *authority* dynamics of teams operating in stressful environments.

The first CRM workshop was held in 1979, sponsored by NASA, and entitled *Resource Management on the Flightdeck*. Workshop discussants agreed that failures of "interpersonal communications, decisionmaking, and leadership,"[89] in particular, were underlying factors in the majority of air crashes to date and training was required. United Airlines took the lead, developing the first comprehensive CRM program in 1981.[90]

Heavily influenced by the thinking of management consultants Robert Blake, an early National Training Laboratories (NTL) enthusiast, and his cofounder of Scientific Methods Inc., Jane Mouton, United's training was based on popular management efficiency programs which had been implemented successfully in a number of major US corporations in the 1970s. NTL was famous for developing inter-personal training programs in the 1950s and 1960s. Sometimes called "personal growth programs," some authors describe this training as "a highly personal approach...deeply rooted in a long history of training—much of which originally had little to do with management or leadership."[91] Instead, training often entailed week-long sessions aimed at learning how one's behavior impacted others and "how to give and receive behavioral feedback." [92] United's program, entitled *Command/Leadership/Resource Management* (C/L/R), was influenced by these popular programs and "emphasized changing *individual* styles and correcting deficiencies in *individual* behavior such as a lack of assertiveness by juniors and authoritarian behavior by captains."[93]

The centerpiece of Blake and Mouton's[94] training approach was the now famous *Managerial Grid* in which participants were asked to respond to a series of survey questions designed to elicit attitudes towards *task* and *people*. For instance, a person with low concern for task accomplishment but high concern for people had a *country club* leadership style. A person with high concern for task accomplishment but low concern for people was considered to have an *authoritarian* leadership style. The training was intended to provide opportunity for participants to reflect on their personal managerial styles and consider how others may perceive their individual behavior in groups.

It was these NTL-based feedback exercises that became notorious amongst pilots. Typically linear thinkers, many pilots were ill equipped emotionally and psychologically to deal with what felt like an onslaught of judgmental, personal criticism masked as "feedback"[95] from peers and subordinates. Unfortunately, many participants were forever alienated by this approach creating staunch critics of the value of leadership and team training programs for high-risk teams.

As a result a new team training model is needed, one that can help professionals in high-risk fields increase their awareness of *four skill areas*: 1) **the dynamics of authority relations; 2) factors affecting the *act of authorizing*; and 3) the interdependent nature of leadership, while 4.) assisting participants to learn how to manage anxiety and continue to think and function in stressful situations.**

CHAPTER V

▼

FOUNDATIONS FOR A NEW TEAM MODEL

🎯 *LEARNING OBJECTIVES*

1. Examine the history of group study.
2. Review the basics of Bion's theories about group behavior.
3. Assess the general premises of the Tavistock method of group study.
4. Clarify how the Tavistock perspective of group study differs from the "personal growth" and "feedback" approach.

Introduction

A review of the past twenty years of CRM programs reveals that although many programs adequately address the first challenge illuminated by the three aviation accidents discussed in chapter four, by improving communication and emphasizing the dangers of non-standard behaviors, **few adequately address the second—how to negotiate the** *dynamics of authority relationships* **and group dynamics in high-risk**

teams. This is because most CRM training programs stress changing individual behaviors rather than learning how to analyze and respond to dynamic *authority* relations in groups.

When leadership and team training does include group dynamics components, it often reflects the theories and methods of the "personal growth" and "feedback" approach, discussed in the last chapter.[96] For example, termed a "re-education" [97] program by National Training Laboratories (NTL) founders, their training focuses on the modification of individual behavior instead of increasing awareness of the authority issues identified previously as central to accidents. They state by positively reinforcing "correct" response and negatively reinforcing "incorrect" responses,[98] their training's goal is to modify participants behavior "toward a more integrative and adaptive interconnection of values, concepts, feelings, perceptions, strategies, and skills." [99]

Yet, as 737 Captain and CRM researcher Gerald Cook noted, professionals in high-risk fields do not always respond well to this format.[100] Therefore, what is needed is a new team training model that can help 1) illuminate the dynamics of authority relations in high-risk teams; 2) expose factors affecting the *act of authorizing*; and 3) examine the interdependent nature of leadership, while 4) supporting participants to learn how to manage anxiety and continue to think and function in stressful situations.

One group study model currently exists which addresses many of these important elements. Originated by the Tavistock Institute of Human Relations in London, the theories and methods underpinning this model are based on group studies done with high-risk teams—military members.[101] Integration of this model into leadership and team training is one way to understand better the dynamics of authority and its impact on high-risk team performance. Although largely developed during and immediately after WWII, the roots of the Tavistock method can actually be traced back to WWI. Let us briefly explore its history and outline key lessons learned.

A Brief History of the Tavistock Approach

World War I

When World War I began, manpower shortages in the United Kingdom exacerbated by significant early battlefield causalities did not allow time to sufficiently screen soldiers. Patriotism was running high and since everyone believed that the war would end quickly, many people responded to the government's massive recruitment efforts, seeing an opportunity to make a wage and eat a hot meal as incentive enough to volunteer. As a result, a good portion of those who enlisted were not fit for military service, let alone the rigorous years of trench warfare that lay ahead.

The cultural climate also compounded problems. In 1914, when war broke out, the British Army was full of career military men, whose character had been shaped by public school[102] ethos, with its clear definitions of duty, honor, loyalty, patriotism and self-sacrifice, thought to epitomize their very identity as Englishmen. With such a strong sense of English character and its corresponding traits of masculinity, it came as quite a shock when, shortly after the war began, large numbers of soldiers from the British Expeditionary Force were evacuated home, apparently suffering from "nervous and mental shock."[103]

The army was ill-prepared to deal with this challenge, which many viewed as cowardliness and a character flaw, and dispatched Cambridge university psychologist, Charles Myers, to the front line to assess the situation. By mid-1916 Myers had seen over 2,000 cases of what became known as *shell-shock*, hypothesized to be the result of an exploding shell's reverberations and explosive gases 'shocking' soldiers' central nervous systems. Especially susceptible, they argued, were nervous soldiers weak in character.[104]

But Myers had different ideas. He discovered that *shell-shocked* soldiers were not always close to a blast. In fact shell-shock often occurred in response to *unexploded* shells, leaving no physical sign of injury. It seemed that the experience of a *near miss* often proved just as psychologically debilitating as actual explosions. As a result, Myers and others, concluded that shell-shock was the inevitable outcome of the stress of trench warfare. Because there were no term limits, soldiers often felt they were sentenced to duty at the front until killed, critically injured or driven crazy by the stress of the environment around them. *Further research determined that every soldier would inevitably break down sooner or later.* Today, we might call this common ailment *post-traumatic stress syndrome.*

World War I taught us a lot about the peculiarities of group dynamics in teams under stress. Although in 1922 the *War Office Committee of Enquiry into 'Shell-Shock'* attempted to consolidate this information, when World War II began less than twenty years later, few preparations had been put in place to address these inevitable challenges.

World War II

A changed Great Britain went reluctantly to war in 1939. The general feeling was more one of dread than the heroic opportunism of the previous war. Although one clear outcome of World War I was recognition of the need for careful screening of recruits, little had been done between the wars to develop a viable process. In particular, was the challenge of developing a more equitable and efficient selection process for officer recruitment. This task was assigned to men commissioned from the Tavistock Clinic in London, an organization founded between the wars based on psychological lessons learned during World War I.

Major Wilfred Bion, a former Tank commander in World War I, made the first of many instrumental contributions by devising the **Leaderless Group**. Perhaps one of the first *experiential* events for high-risk teams, candidates were given a task, such as building a bridge, and then observed to see to what extent they were able to maintain personal relationships under the stress. Would an officer candidate, for instance, disregard the interests of his team in favor of satisfying his own needs as stress intensified? This new selection process proved extremely successful, not only increasing recruitment numbers by 1,500%,[105] but by also selecting better qualified soldiers, restoring faith in the officer selection process and helping create a less class-ridden, more skill-based *New Army.*

Although senior army leaders preferred to ignore the psychological toll the war was exacting, new research revealed *good leadership* had tremendous influence over the number of shell-shock cases a unit suffered. For instance, units lead by strong commanders often had fewer psychological casualties while other units, involved in the same battle led by different commanders, almost entirely broke down.

For most soldiers it was not outdated notions of English character that kept them fighting, as previously imagined, but rather it was loyalty to their group—their unit, hometown and families—that motivated them onwards, helping them contain the chaos of the environment around them. Any break in this support chain, such as a "Dear John" letter from home or the death of a unit leader, increased the chance of psychological breakdown. As a result, rules of rotation were developed for the first time: American troops were limited to 210 days of fighting while the British adopted a policy of 400 days, rotating soldiers off the front line for 4 days rest every 12 duty days.[106]

Post-World War II

The post-World War II period could be classified as the birth era of the field of group study as many people excitedly experimented with the knowledge gained from their wartime experiences.[107] Central to this exploration were that of Bion and his fellow members of the Tavistock Clinic, then Tavistock Institute, in England and Kurt Lewin and the National Training Laboratory (NTL) in America. The NTL's contributions proved pivotal with the development of its human laboratory, an experiential method of studying groups in the *here-and-now*, in 1947.

In London, Bion continued making significant contributions to social psychiatry. In 1948, he was asked *to take* therapeutic groups, a colloquialism for employing the group techniques he had honed through his experiences in World War II. While working with this small group of patients in the adult department of the Tavistock Clinic, Bion decided to provide the group with no direction and no structure in order to assess the group's reaction.

One author observed that the reason for this abrupt break from traditional methods was twofold: "First, he wasn't sure what he was doing so he decided to remain silent. Second, he [was] a rather withdrawn individual."[108] As a result of Bion's silence, the patients were puzzled, upset and angry and responded in a variety of ways. Bion's unique contribution was that he interpreted these reactions not as the behavior of individual group members, but as the *group's dynamic as a whole.*

What may have started as a response to uncertainty and/or a reflection of Bion's personality was transformed eventually into a consulting technique central to the Tavistock tradition. A fellow Tavistock colleague, Eric Trist wrote the following observation of Bion's methods for taking groups:

> Several features characterized Bion's group 'style'. He was detached yet warm, utterly imperturbable and inexhaustibly patient. He gave rise to feelings of immense security—his Rock of Gibraltar quality. But the Rock of Gibraltar is also powerful and he exuded power (he was also a very large man).[109]

In psychological terms, Bion seemed to be inviting, whether consciously or not, the group's *projective identification* with him. That is, he made himself available for the group to disown their uncomfortable feelings and project them onto him as a means to understand the group's unconscious behavior. As Trist put it, "He made it safe for the group to dramatize its unconscious situation."[110]

Bion's Theories

As previously discussed, Bion's methods were heavily influenced by the theories of psychoanalyst Melanie Klein, especially her ideas about basic defense mechanisms called *splitting* and *projective identification.* Klein studied infants, developing a theory that babies reconcile conflicts between its perception of the nurturing and satisfying mother and the frustrating and withholding mother by *splitting* the mother into two separate *objects*, as discussed previously in chapter one. The infant then perceives one object to be 'nurturing' and 'good' and the other object as 'frustrating' and 'bad'. Similarly, the infant learns to distance itself psychologically from its own negative and destructive emotions by disowning uncomfortable feelings and *projecting* them onto someone else.

These theories—*splitting* and *projective identification*—proved to be the link Bion needed to join theories describing the *individual's* unconscious experience with those he was developing to represent experiences of *group* membership. Bion extended Klein's theories by exploring how group membership often evoked some of the very same contradictory feelings as those the baby experienced during childhood in response to the mother. Through Bion's lens, Klein's object relations theory explained how experiences in groups trigger "primitive *phantasies* whose origins lie in the earliest years of life."[111] For example, one unconscious desire is for the individual to join with others in an undifferentiated entity, like the infant fusing with the mother. Although comforting, this desire also creates resultant fears, such as the fear of becoming overwhelmed or consumed by the undifferentiated mass of the group or the fear of being rejected or abandoned by the group.

Although over fifty years old, Bion's theories remain relevant and continue to be interpreted and evolved by other social scientists both inside and outside the Tavistock Institute in their continued exploration of how best to understand groups and organizations.

Development of the Tavistock Method

The Tavistock Institute was an exciting place after World War II where many social scientists collaborated to put lessons learned from wartime to new use in peacetime organizations.[112] The Institute was established as a charitable not-for-profit with the goal to provide "collaborative services" and undertake "studies concerned with human relations in the family, the factory, and the community."[113] They based their work on three principles: "First and foremost, a therapeutic approach to human problems;" second, the integration of "medical and social studies…through the insights of psychoanalysis;" and third, a "devotion to social action and related research and training."[114]

Central to this perspective was the Institute staff's belief that changes in ones environment had a direct impact on circumstances contributing to people's mental health and well being.[115] In other words, based on wartime studies that had determined that *all* soldiers would eventually breakdown, Institute staff were intrigued by how environmental stressors might affect individuals' emotional experience and productivity. **They were interested, in particular, in the interplay between social and technical elements within one's environment.**

Yet these progressive thinkers were not alone. During this time, powerful individual contributions occurred both in the U.S. and UK, influencing this exciting post-war period. In the U.S., Kurt Lewin's work with Ronald Lippitt, Kenneth Benne and Leland Bradford, and the emergence of the *human interaction laboratory* during a 1946 *Connecticut Workshop in Human Relations*, had worldwide impact. In the UK, Bion's theories about people's behavior in groups and other socio-technical projects being pursued by Trist, Bridger, Rice, Jaques and Menzies at the Institute, also were influential.

The *Group Relations Conference*

One example of this cross-pollination between American and British group theorists and the application of the newly emerging Tavistock theories and methods was the development of the first *group relations conference* held at the University of Leicester in 1957, colloquially referred to as the *Leicester Conference* or simply *Leicester*. Eric J. Miller, director of the Tavistock Institute's Group Relations Training Programme (1970-1996) noted, "The first Leicester Conference was explicitly a British 'translation' of NTL, using Bion's group-as-a-whole perspective from group psychotherapy."[116] In addition Eric Trist, director of the Institute's first *Leicester Conference*, noted that this event was "the first full-scale experiment in Britain with the 'laboratory' method of training in group relations."[117] Miller described how this reference to "the laboratory method" was an obvious credit to Lewin, the NTL and its *human interaction laboratory* method "which had strongly influenced the early Tavistock group."[118]

In addition to evidence that the *Leicester Conference* design incorporated theories and methods adapted from NTL, there is evidence that the Tavistock Institute adopted NTL terminology as well. For instance, in 1959, Trist and Sofer published a report of the first Leicester Conference and in it often used NTL-like language—e.g. *laboratory, here-and-now*, and *social islands*—when describing Tavistock's *group relations conference* events. All of these terms were made famous a decade earlier in Bethel, Maine by Lewin and his followers at the NTL.

Yet, despite evidence of early cross-pollination, Tavistock and NTL models soon began to diverge as differences emerged, which would later become defining trends for these separate models. For example the NTL's focus at the individual level rather than *group-as-a-whole*, its focus on scientific research methods and lack of awareness of psychoanalytic principles caused Institute staff to question future collaborations. Instead, the Tavistock Institute put its energies into developing their own model and its application in the *group relations conference*.

The *group relations conference* was the amalgamation of Institute staff's wartime experiences with officer selection and *Leaderless Groups*, Civil Resettlement Units, therapeutic communities and Lewin and NTL's *human interaction laboratory*. Deemed a 'pilot study' this event was the first of many conferences designed to study inter-personal and inter-group relations within the isolation of a 'cultural island'. Since 1957, thousands of events such as this have occurred worldwide based on similar principles, including the one in which you will soon participate.

The Tavistock Method

The general premise of the Tavistock method is to study a group or organization as a whole entity, not as a disconnected set of individuals. In contrast to NTL's interpersonal perspective, the Tavistock approach refocuses the level of analysis on covert group processes—the often unspoken dynamics of *authority* within the group—and considers *authority* not as an individual's characteristics but as **patterns of relationship found in the group-as-a-whole**. Rather than relying on NTL-feedback exercises, which may lead to individual resistance, the Tavistock approach aims to expose the realities of the messy, conflict-ridden complexity of group life. This approach provides no easy measures for understanding one's *managerial style*. Instead, it assumes that groups work in cyclic, not linear, ways oscillating from anxiety modes to work modes and back again, and focuses on heightening the group's awareness of individual psychology, group dynamics and systemic factors so that teams can operate more effectively.

One might ask: NTL—interpersonal; Tavistock—group-as-a-whole; why does it matter which perspective to employ in team training? The answer lies in where responsibility is placed—in other words, *who is authorized*—to make changes within the system. Are individuals made to feel *personally* responsible and defensive leading to perceptions of being attacked, ridiculed or judged? Or, as Majors Wilfred Bion and John Rickman[119] proposed during their group study at Northfield Hospital during World War II, are team failures seen as a disability of the community-as-a-whole?[120]

Although both the NTL and Tavistock models are based on *experiential* pedagogy, such as investigating the group as a microcosm of society, studying behavior as it occurs in the here-and-now, and providing opportunities for individuals to interpret their own learning experience, the two models emphasize distinctly different behaviors.[121] For example, the pedagogy employed at many current CRM training events is one in which participants are provided feedback in order to help diagnose and experiment with their own behavior and relationships during group learning activities. More specifically, these NTL-influenced models focus on modifying an individual's directly observable behaviors and attitudes through a variety of feedback exercises.[122]

In contrast, the Tavistock model's *group relations events* provide opportunities to examine covert, unconscious group behaviors especially in relation to *authority* figures, within a temporary social institution.[123] This model fosters the study of *authority*, and the obvious and not-so-obvious dynamics which influence the success and failure of leadership efforts, such as the glaring deficiencies illuminated in the previously discussed aviation accidents. Understanding *authority* and how it influences people's behavior in groups must become a central concept in **Team Resource Management (TRM)** programs.

Heightening **TRM** trainees' awareness of covert processes at the *group-as-a-whole* level enables them to understand better the systemic influences on the group's decisionmaking capacity, better preparing them to take responsibility for their behavior as a group. Ironically, by focusing on the group's dynamics and shifting attention away from the individual, individual leadership capacities are fostered. In other words, increased awareness of the group-as-a-whole enables trainees to learn to manage themselves in the multiple roles necessary for contemporary leadership by encouraging critical thinking about the covert processes which can influence the success or failure of leadership efforts.

▼

CHAPTER VI

TEAM RESOURCE MANAGEMENT (TRM) MODEL

 **LEARNING OBJECTIVES**

1. Identify the three non-linear forces that affect high-risk team processes.
2. Provide examples of the three non-linear forces from your organizational experiences.
3. Identify the four TRM elements.
4. Clarify the definition of *Team Resource Management (TRM)*.

Introduction

For the most part people living in the western world, Americans in particular, have grown accustomed to quick fix plans and short-lived fads. Whether in the form of the latest diet, fitness routine or managerial strategy, Americans are *comfortable* when presented with the "seven habits" or "twelve steps" required for change processes yet often *uncomfortable* acknowledging complexity and dealing with the messiness of in-process dynamics.

Therefore, it is not surprising that many American researchers studying group life adopted some form of *stages* of group development. For instance, Tuckman and Jensen called their stages of team development *forming, storming, norming, performing* and *adjourning*. Although nearly thirty years old, this approach remains popular in US group study literature because Americans often crave easy solutions to complex problems.[124]

It is also not surprising that personality measurements, such as the Minnesota Multiphasic Personality Inventory (MMPI), Blake and Mouton's *Managerial Grid*, or Myers-Briggs Type Indicator (MBTI) remain popular. These measures are statistically valid and reliable, and often part of CRM training programs, satisfying trainers' fantasies that if the right personalities have been identified and grouped together, the team will be effective. Yet, such approaches ignore the fact that ***people behave differently in different groups and team dynamics often move in unpredictably complex—not reliably linear—ways.*** So what then would experts recommend high-risk team training entail?

Criteria for High-Risk Team Training

Dozens of books have been written about teams in the past decade, books entitled "team-building," "the discipline of teams," "overcoming the five dysfunctions of a teams," "leading teams," "the 17 essential qualities," and the "wisdom of teams," for example.[125] Although this list is a positive indication of people's growing interest in the topic, few authors agree on which factors are essential. Even in high-risk organizations such as airlines, armed forces, nuclear plants and law enforcement, where the repercussions of mistakes can be catastrophic, leadership and team training criteria remain vague.

For example, although the Federal Aviation Administration (FAA) has endorsed *human factors training* for years, they remain reluctant to dictate specific criteria for team training programs. FAA documents highlight historical deficiencies, noting that **pilot training programs have overly focused on technical skills and individual competence and "did not effec-**

tively address crew management issues that are also fundamental to safe flight."126 Yet they stop short of providing explicit training guidance. As a result, numerous perspectives on high-risk team training have emerged within the aviation field such as Command/Leadership/Resource Management (C/L/R), Aircrew Coordination Training (ACT) or the more commonplace Crew Resource Management (CRM).

Without specific training criteria, how are high-risk teams expected to gain many of the skills deemed essential to safe and efficient operation? Just like the FAA example above, the culture in many high-risk organizations supports that as individuals gain operational or field experience, rising through the organizational ranks, they will naturally acquired the requisite leadership, communication and teambuilding skills in order to succeed. In this environment, people often believe that what new employees need is technical training and strict evaluation of these skills through individual measures of competence. They mistakenly believe new employees will have time to acquire the 'people skills' later, on the job.

Yet, more and more we find team skill-building does not occur. Instead, in many high-risk environments, team skills become devalued in favor of technical competence and individual prowess. In part because there is a need for training aimed at putting foundational building blocks in place, but also because the organizational climate is resistant, team skills may become undervalued. Under such circumstances, once a professional has become technically qualified in their field, they are often thrust into leadership roles in response to operational necessity, only then realizing the gaps in their skills and training.

To understand the complex set of factors affecting performance of teams in a high-risk environment, I have developed a model called *Team Resource Management (TRM)*. Although the essential elements of the *TRM* model are described in this *Primer*, *TRM* is not something one can learn simply by reading about it. Like any new skill, once given tools through preliminary instruction, one must put them into practice in order to develop appropriate mastery. Therefore, participants will be given opportunities to test their *TRM* skills in a number of experiential exercises. Before we discuss the exercises, let us examine the elements of the *TRM* model.

The *TRM* Model[127]

> **TRM Defined:** *TRM* is a sense-making process designed
> to expose and manage team errors and conflicts as they
> shape *authority* relations in a dynamic context.

Rooted in *socio-technical* change management processes, the *TRM* model emphasizes proper identification, assessment and application of all available resources—information, equipment and people—in pursuit of safe and efficient operations in high-risk teams. The *socio-technical system perspective*, first developed by the Tavistock Institute through their work in British coal-mines in the 1940s and '50s, provides a way to optimize both human elements and technological capacities within organizations without subverting either.[128]

Prior to development of the *socio-technical* perspective in the post-World War II period, industries often emphasized either people or machines when implementing new developments, rarely considering the overall impact of one on the other. For instance, Tavistock researchers found that although new coal mining equipment was available, "productivity failed to increase in step with increases in mechanization."[129] In other words, **as industries became more mechanized and technologically advanced, output actually *decreased* as employee turnover, absenteeism and labor disputes increased taking their toll on productivity.**

These enhanced technological developments often had an inverse relationship to overall productivity as workers struggled to adjust to changes in their work environment. Typically, management's response to worker dissatisfaction was to improve worker compensation and benefits paying little attention to the psychological aspect of employee's work experience.

Tavistock Institute researchers were not alone in their endeavors to understand better the interplay between the worker and his or her environment. Other scholars had been intrigued by the impact of the work environment on employee performance. One of the first theorists to apply psychology to the workplace, *Mary Parker Follett* described the advantages of a more cooperative work environment in her essay *The Giving of Orders* in 1926. Arguing for a less hierarchical worker-management interface, Follett offered that the solution to workers' resistance to following orders was to "depersonalize the giving of orders."[130] Perhaps one of the first to propose a *collaborative* work environment, she suggested that workers and foremen study a situation together; allowing a solution to emerge naturally, calling this *scientific management.*

Between 1927 and 1932, ***Elton Mayo*** conducted a now famous study at the Hawthorne Works of the Western Electric Company in Chicago. By studying women assembling telephone relays, Mayo explored the link between human motivation and productivity.[131] "The *Hawthorne experiments* showed that complex, interactional variables make the difference in motivating people—things like attention paid to workers as individuals, workers' control over their own work, differences between individuals' needs, management's willingness to listen, group norms, and direct feedback."[132] The contributions of Follett and Mayo paved the way for the development of new theories recognizing organizations as complex interactive systems, highlighting the importance of considering "the human aspect of industry."[133]

As a result of these and other studies, "*a new paradigm of work*"[134] emerged which considered the work system as a whole and work groups within it, instead of focusing only on individual workers and their performance. In the past, researcher's found management assumed that all people-, or *socio-*, problems could be overcome by greater financial compensation, treating each worker like a *technical,* interchangeable machine part. Tavistock Institute researchers argued that both socio- and technical factors must be taken into account in efforts to improve organizational life and productivity. Subsequent research in hospitals and cotton mills produced similar results. These innovations directly influenced post-war theories about industrial democracy, spawning an international *quality of work-life movement*, particularly popular in the US and Scandinavian countries.[135]

This *socio-technical, paradigm of work* underpins the *TRM* model. In other words, it assumes that to improve the operations of high-risk teams, one must improve both the socio-factors such as psychological expectations, organizational culture, and group norms and values, as well as the technical-factors such as modern equipment and proper training.

Group-as-a-Whole

In addition to the *socio-technical paradigm of work*, another important contribution from Tavistock Institute researchers was development of the *group-as-a-whole* perspective and its application through the Tavistock approach to group study. This method stresses that when examining peoples' behavior in groups, it is not only possible but essential to identify behaviors that express the life of the *group-as-a-whole* entity. From this perspective, the *group-as-a-whole* is capable of expressing feelings and thoughts through individual group members as well as causing actions such as scapegoating and groupthink, described in chapter two.

For example, if an individual becomes so bored or agitated by the group's activities he or she leaves the room, one interpretation could be that the *group-as-a-whole* played a part in ejecting this member from the group for some reason. Perhaps this member was felt to be 'different,' slow the group down or represent an uncomfortable dynamic that the group was not yet ready to address. Before the individual departed, the group may have been subtly—or not so subtly—'*acting as if*' only that person would leave; then the group could get back on task. As a sign of the group's 'relief,' one group member may comment that they are "glad he's gone." This comment, although voiced by one individual, is interpreted to be made on behalf of the entire *group-as-a-whole*. In other words, the *group* is happy to be rid of the ejected group member—not just the individual who stated it. Analyzing the role individuals play on behalf of the *group-as-a-whole* is an important aspect of the Tavistock approach to group study.

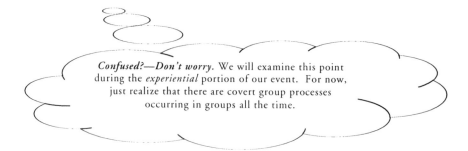

Confused?—Don't worry. We will examine this point during the *experiential* portion of our event. For now, just realize that there are covert group processes occurring in groups all the time.

Of course, at one level, it is nonsensical to talk about a *group* feeling something, for the feelings reside in and are actually felt by the members of the group." [136] However, there are certain experiences and sensations that are different when experienced within groups than in isolation, and can be identified as a representation of the *group-as-a-whole*. Although these feelings may in fact be only 'voiced' by a certain faction of the group, we consider this sub-group to be speaking on behalf of the entire *group-as-a-whole*. You will be exposed to this perspective during the experiential events. For now, just understand that individuals' behavior can be considered a group dynamic.

How Does *Group-as-a-Whole* Apply to *TRM*?

How does *group-as-a-whole* apply to *TRM*? Unlike other team training models, *TRM* refocuses the level of analysis on the covert group processes, the often unspoken dynamics of the group, which operate not at the level of individual distinctions, but at the level of the *group-as-a-whole*. By identifying and assessing both obvious and not-so-obvious influences on team performance, *TRM* can help overcome obstacles to effective teamwork thereby reducing errors and miscommunications in high-risk industries.

TRM does not claim to provide easy measures or finite steps to team-building success but rather aims to expose people to the realities of the messy, conflict-ridden complexity of group life. This approach assumes that groups work in cyclic, not linear, ways oscillating from anxiety modes to work modes and back again. *TRM* promises no easy steps or personality measures to ensure team success. Rather, it focuses on strategies to heighten the group's awareness of *individual psychology*, *group dynamics* and *systemic* factors so that teams can operate more effectively in a wide range of areas.

The common goal of team training must be for everyone within the organizational system as a whole to *recognize the existence of team failures as a disability of the entire community and not simply the failure of individual members within it.* By increasing awareness of the dynamics of *authority*, people should become less afraid to take up *authority* and act.

TRM is distinct because it strives to uncover the complex ways individuals, teams, groups and organizations interact with their environment. Similar to previous team-training models, there are a number of basic elements that help structure the training process. But, unlike other programs, these elements are not introduced in a linear or self-limiting fashion. Instead, as the *TRM* diagram depicts, this training explores how different elements combine in complex ways, reflecting the continuous interaction among individuals, groups and systems.

Figure 1 represents the three interdependent tornadoes of the *TRM* model. This diagram depicts the *three non-linear forces in process (individual psychology, group dynamics* and *systems* theory) with the *four elements* (leadership, communication, teamwork and sense-making) of the *TRM* model in a Venn diagram.

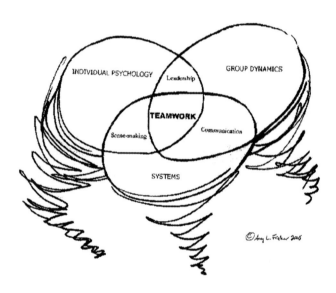

Figure 1.

The *Three Non-Linear Forces in Process*

The TRM model incorporates three non-linear forces which constantly influence the performance of high-risk teams: *individual psychology, group dynamics* and *systemic* factors. The following section describes these forces and how they can have an impact on team performance.

Individual Psychology and *Group Dynamics*

When a person is involved in organizational or group life, she or he is influenced both by the external environment of the work setting, as well as by their own internal environment, largely a product of previous experiences such as work, school, family and childhood.[137] In other words, as humans we naturally compare our current experiences with those previously encountered. This comparison is often unconscious, such as when we unexpectedly find ourselves attracted to, or repelled by, people or places which subtly 'remind us' of something else.

As a result, anxiety stimulated by memories of past experiences can evoke primitive reactions of competition, envy, dependency, aggression, sympathy, love and hope in individuals; feelings whose seeds were planted years before. These powerful undercurrents are often invisible to the individuals in whom they are evoked, yet can have an impact on group dynamics as others within the team or organization sense them.[138]

"The tendency for most human beings to *split* the good from the bad in themselves and to *project* their resultant feelings upon others is one of the major barriers to the understanding and control of behaviour."[139] This means that any time people come together in groups, individuals' feelings, reactions and defenses can get activated in service to the group. These uncomfortable feelings can get *split* off and *projected* onto others, as described previously. Particularly appealing targets for these unwanted feelings are people taking up *authority* roles.

Recall from previous discussions that one of the *leadership* tasks of people in *authority roles* is to regulate the *boundary* region.[140] In other words, good leaders create an environment that enables work to be accomplished by allowing enough exchange with the environment to avoid creating a closed system, but not so much that chaos overwhelms the organization with outside input. As a result when work is not accomplished effectively, a natural tendency is for groups to blame people in *authority* roles. *Splitting* off their own uncomfortable feelings of failure, disappointment, anger and shame, groups project these feelings on to authority figures, thereby dis-owning their own responsibility.

Conversely, people in *authority roles* can also *split* off their feelings of frustration and *project* them onto groups within their organization. As dis-cussed previously, the organization acts as if these all-bad departments or individuals are the cause of all the organization's troubles. The CEO or human resource director thinks, '*If only* these troublemakers would go away, everything would be fine.' An example of this phenomenon is described below.

An Example of Organizational Conflict

Research consultants were asked to investigate an organizational con-flict occurring within the Buildings and Maintenance Division of a mid-sized state hospital. Observing what he thought was a personality conflict between two employees, the frustrated division director instructed the consultants, "I want you to go down to Design and Engineering and *fix the women*."[141]

The consultants accepted the challenge and began their work by invit-ing staff to meet with them as a sign of collaboration. Yet, after the meet-ing they noted, "We had never seen a group of employees be so open in expressing bitterness, cruelty, and contempt for one another."[142] Although surprised they remained hopeful because, since the conflict surfaced in public, at least it could be addressed and they set about gathering more data. Surprisingly, the consultants found that the tensions between the two women *troublemakers* "were tame compared to the emotions" others attached to the conflict.[143] In other words, the *group-as-a-whole* seemed much more invested in perpetuating the 'women's conflict' than the women themselves did.

For example, out of the women's earshot, many of the organization's key "men seemed to delight in telling" stories and half-truths about the combat-ive duo, thereby escalating the conflict. "The other men condoned" these unprofessional comments "as if it were merely 'locker-room' banter among 'the guys.'"[144] Yet, these dynamics aroused researchers' interest; "what pur-poses of the men were being served by the two women's clashes?"[145]

What they discovered was that the unit had three informal, covert cliques, each led by a strong male authority figure. Unresolved interpersonal tensions and competitiveness among these three powerful men were being driven into the relationships between the cliques and were *projected* onto the conflict between the women. "The volatile affect of the cliques was being expressed by women in the unit, thereby giving the men a means to release their emotions vicariously yet appear calm and detached from the conflict."[146] The director mistook the anxiety caused by unresolved competition between the men and their cliques as interpersonal conflict between two women. He mistakenly thought, "*If only* these consultants could 'fix the women' everything would be fine."

In the Tenerife example discussed previously, we saw other examples of these phenomena in both the intimidated KLM co-pilot and the impatient KLM captain. For example, the co-pilot seemed overly influenced by the impressive credentials and authoritarian demeanor of the experience KLM captain, allowing the captain's authority effectively to silence him. Perhaps recalling previous experiences of feeling vulnerable, the copilot did not want to display his inexperience in the aircraft, and allowed the captain to takeoff even though he seemed to know it was unsafe. The KLM captain, growing frustrated with the numerous delays and communication problems, was impatient and projected these frustrations onto others around him. The captain's impatience further flustered the Dutch co-pilot as his English radio communications became more and more ambiguous.

Although identifying and understanding these covert dynamics is important for successful high-risk team performance, most team training only obliquely engages with the topic. In existing CRM training models, the phenomenon described above might be called principles of good judgment, effective decision making, or awareness of hazardous attitudes. The essence of these concepts focuses on the individual's "perception" of what's going on and "the ability to distinguish between correct and incorrect solutions."[147] Rarely does training address that **there might be multiple, correct perceptions of reality occurring, thereby revealing the challenge for high-risk teams to learn to negotiate through conflict.** Surfacing conflicts—not avoiding them—is one way to improve team performance in high-risk fields. In other words, once one accepts that group life is complex, not linear, and influenced by a number of powerful yet unseen variables, it becomes clear that high-risk teams need a complex 'toolbox' of skills in order to be effective.

Another Example of Individual Psychology and Group Dynamics

Although CRM training has grown popular, spreading to a number of other high-risk industries over the years, very little CRM training provides opportunities for participants to increase their awareness of *authority* relationships and *group-as-a-whole* dynamics. In fact, in my experience, training almost exclusively focuses on the individualistic perspective discussed previously.

For example, as a commercial airline pilot I was once involved in a two day CRM-like training[148] workshop where senior captains and copilots were asked to participate in a role-playing event. The task my group was assigned was to determine the best course of action given the following scenario:

> "In Flight Operations, a male Captain and female First Officer were flight-planning. At a table next to them a couple of fellow pilots loudly made several derogatory comments about women pilots. The First Officer was the only female in Flight Ops."[149]

The solution to this problem seemed obvious to me, a female first officer: It was clearly an issue of *authority.*

All eyes immediately turned to me, the only women in the group. Yet, I initially restrained from engaging in the discussion. The men in the group quickly and unanimously agreed that the fellow pilots' "derogatory comments about women pilots" were inappropriate. Yet, they thought that the female first officer, even though she was "the only female in Flight Ops," should be the person to correct the inappropriate behavior. "If she's offended," one man noted "*she* should say something," as if there were no other covert group dynamics present. I tried to explain that the female first officer was in many ways the *least authorized—and most vulnerable to scape-goating*—if she took up this challenge. Yet, the male pilots present could not understand. Even though many admitted they would be offended if they heard the inappropriate comments themselves, they did not assume they had any responsibility to intervene. In other words, they lacked a way to comprehend *group-as-a-whole* dynamics or their collusion within the system. One senior male Line Check Captain candidly reasoned "I don't want to become the hall monitor for the entire pilot population."

Just as in the KLM Tenerife accident, the majority demanded that members of the least authorized group, and therefore most powerless, challenge the system; they lacked awareness of the systemic interdependence of members of the group.

Systems Thinking

Many early theorists, such as "Hegel, Marx, Schopenhauer, Nietzsche, Spengler, Spencer, to mention a few,"[150] made contributions to our understanding of *whole systems*, laying an intellectual foundation for general inquiry into the nature of social systems. Similar to *TRM's* tornado forces, the premise of systems thinking is that there are a multitude of complex forces simultaneously influencing systems of organizational life. Therefore, **in order to understand a group's behaviors one must examine not only an organization's structure, products and services, policies and procedures, and methods of remuneration and reward, but also group members' fears, anxieties, values, hopes and beliefs.**

Several early Tavistock Institute studies[151] showed how **organizations develop mechanisms to defend against the anxiety inherent in the system, both alleviating and exacerbating the anxiety of members within it.** These defense mechanisms are methods to help an organization's members deal with "disturbing emotional experiences—methods which are built into the way the organization works."[152]

For example, in the 1950s Jaques observed how *splitting*, idealization and denial occurred on a massive scale within a factory called Glacier Metals. Workers *split* mangers into good and bad categories while managers idealized the worker-manager relationship, denying any conflict existed between the two groups, feeding a vicious emotional cycle of *projective identification.*

In another important study, Menzies Lyth found hospitals often develop procedures not aimed at improving patient care but rather to contain staffs' anxiety about working with sick and dying patients. For example, rather than developing ways to confront and vent job induced anxiety, Menzies Lyth found that a social defense system emerged that actually exacerbated nurses' anxiety leading to high turnover and burnout along with low morale and job satisfaction.

More recently Hirshhorn used his experience as an organizational consultant to identify other examples of this phenomenon in organizations such as nuclear plants, government agencies and various businesses. He observed that **anxiety in organizations trigger primitive fears of annihilation** resulting in the creation of social defenses, just as Jaques and Menzies noted.

Yet, Hirshhorn identified two new modes of social defense: *organizational rituals* and **covert coalitions.** *Organizational rituals* are depersonalized routines that allow individuals to distance themselves from the anxiety created by their role. Yet this depersonalization also reduces emotional connections in the workplace, replacing them with mechanized routines. *Covert coalitions* constitute an often unspoken psychological contract where people agree not to talk about certain *taboo* subjects, thereby perpetuating a dysfunctional climate within the organization.[153] In both cases, fear of escalating anxiety results in a connectionless environment prone to *splitting* and other defenses.

In my research, I examined defenses that became activated within a commercial airline in the US in the immediate post-9/11 time period considering, in particular, the debate surrounding arming airline pilots with handguns. I argued that high levels of fear, guilt, anxiety and an overwhelming sense of responsibility for elements often outside their sphere of control led airline pilots to feel isolated, lonely, hopeless, and inadequate in the weeks and months following 9/11. As they struggled to regain their personal sense of security, control, and prestige many pilots felt pressured from a number of sources to be armed as the "last line of defense" against a terrorist attack onboard their aircraft.[154]

Analyzing these studies, two training strategies become clear: First, successful high-risk teams need people who can identify, confront and vent anxieties, rather than becoming debilitated by them, and either thoughtlessly jumping to action or seeking to scapegoat; Second, organizations need to develop a more inclusive culture that accepts complexity, tolerates ambiguity, surfaces conflict and supports a learning process at all levels in order to manage organizational anxiety.[155]

How can one learn these strategies? I would argue one learns to mobilize uncertainty and complexity to enhance, rather than preclude leadership, communication, teamwork and sense-making in high-risk teams.

The Four *TRM* Elements

Now that we have an understanding of the three non-linear forces in process that effect all teams and organizations—*individual psychology, group dynamics* and *systemic* factors—we can explore the *four core TRM elements*. These *four core elements* are *leadership, communication* and *sense-making* which intersect to form *teamwork* in the TRM diagram. Each element will be discussed in the following section.

I. Leadership

Leadership theories and methods of evaluating leadership effectiveness were discussed in depth in earlier chapters. In this section we focus on application, examining how one can exercise leadership effectively in a high-risk team.

TRM philosophy does not support the idea that a team has only one leader. Rather, TRM supports the concept that an effective team shares the leadership role. This is not to say that there is *no* leader, but that each team member has leadership potential. And, depending on the team's task, the team allows the most qualified individual to lead as required. If a team has a number of tasks to managed, as most teams do, each member may share the leadership role to accomplish them.

Clear *authority roles* still remain—a police chief, military officer or airline captain does not relinquish this *authority role* or the corresponding responsibility. Yet, depending on the nature of a team's task, the person occupying the *formal* authority role may not be the most suitable leader at all times and can relinquish leadership to a better suited teammate.

For example, a police lieutenant may be in charge of a large scale undercover operation. On the day of the arrest, it may become clear during the team briefing that the lieutenant, although the senior officer, is not as familiar with the building's layout as some of the other officers. As a result, these officers may take a more active leadership role, managing tasks that need to be accomplished, while the lieutenant steps back and accepts a less prominent leadership role. The lieutenant never relinquishes her *formal authority role*, but shares leadership with individuals best suited for the task.

II. Communication

Communication is sometimes called the glue that holds the team process together, and enables implementation of the other *TRM* elements.[156] Yet, its complexity is often a misunderstood and undervalued skill in high-risk professions. For instance, we often think of communication in an all-or-nothing way—we are either understood or misunderstood, persuaded or unmoved, agreed or disagree with—ignoring the fact that there is much ambiguity and innuendo in the communication process.[157] In fact words are only a small part of the communication process. A large part of communication is conveyed via body language and other non-verbal means.

Since communication is the process by which we exchange information with others, it can be understood as influenced by three key factors: 1) The sender, 2) receiver and 3) message. The personality, background and perceived character of the sender have a significant impact on the communication process. Recipients are constantly judging whether the sender seems credible or trustworthy and whether the message is believable. Since people tend to be attracted to others who possess similar characteristics, come from similar backgrounds or represent a group they aspire to join, demographics play a pivotal role in this judgment.[158] Identity characteristics such as race, gender, sexual orientation, religion, age, height, weight, attractiveness, professional experience, hobbies, family connections, friendships and a list of other factors, all become influential as recipients decide how much *authority* to award the sender and his or her message.

Recipients of the communication are not the only ones judging, the sender must also assess the intelligence, language skills, expectations and personality characteristics of the intended audience. For instance, when collaborating with professionals from different organizations the effective communicator must be wary of alienating others through the use of professional jargon not easily understood. He or she should also consider the audience's potential reaction to the message when choosing words. Is this a message that was expected and generally agreed with, or is it difficult news for the recipients to hear?

Many high-risk team models of communication still reflect a *centralized*, command-and-control paradigm, emphasizing communication as the exchange of "information" and "instructions" from one leader to recipients in a manner which they can clearly and correctly understand.[159] Yet **if effective high-risk teams operate in a more *decentralized* fashion, sharing the leadership role depending on the task, then communication becomes a complex *act of authorizing*.**

Consider whose words get heard and recalled during stressful conditions. Often it is people who have been awarded *authority*, whether formally or informally, by the group. Reflect on your group and organizational experiences. Have you ever offered an important insight or idea that was initially ignored until someone else repeated it?

Five Ways Effective High-Risk Teams Use Communication

There are at least five ways that effective communication is essential to high-risk teams' effective performance in the operational environment, and they often occur simultaneously: 1) information exchange; 2) establishing work-oriented interpersonal relationships; 3) establishing predictable behavior patterns; 4) maintaining attention to task; and 5) establishing leadership.[160]

First, the *TRM* model supports that it is a team's collective responsibility to establish and maintain a professional climate, a climate of curiosity and open communication to ensure the ***successful exchange of information***. The professionalism of a team can be improved by engaging honestly and respectfully, soliciting feedback, appreciating people's efforts and avoiding inappropriate jokes or slang. By keeping the climate professional, teammates stay open to learning from experience, creating an environment that is conducive to innovation, growth and creativity.

Second, by collectively creating and maintaining a professional climate the high-risk ream can ***establish work-oriented interpersonal relationships***. Conversely, in an unprofessional climate, people often feel uncomfortable and grow mistrustful, interested more in self-preservation than creating a healthy team environment. Rather than committing to the team's vision, recognizing there is a collective, interdependence to their relationship, organizing in a systemic way, and sharing leadership roles, individuals begin to act more like a crowd—interested in only satisfying their own needs and desires.

Third, although high-risk teams establish ***predictable behavior patterns*** through the use of manuals, checklists, standard operating procedures and training it is also important to have a common language that can flag areas of concern as they emerge. For example, TRM uses *'CUS' words*—the words *concern, uncomfortable* and *safety*—as communication red flags that things are not going well. In the Portland crash discussed previously, the copilot might have drawn the captain's attention by stating "Captain, I'm *concerned* about the low fuel situation and feel it's *unsafe* to proceed. We need to land now." Through the use of this common phraseology, all crewmembers understand that there is an important safety concern being expressed which needs to be addressed as soon as possible.

Fourth, in addition to 'CUS' words, *TRM* endorses a method called *The Big Three—inquiry, advocacy,* and *assertiveness*—as a communication strategy to maintain team members' ***attention to task***. When a team member feels concerned or uncomfortable about an unfolding event, the first step is to clearly state what is being experienced and **inquire** if other team members are experiencing the same thing. In other words, compare the inside experience with the outside world by communicating with the group to determine reality. A copilot might *inquire,* "Do you always fly the approach into this airport this low, captain?"

If an adequate response is not received, the next step is to **advocate** a plan of action in a clear and articulate manner. Avoiding fuzzy phrases, slang and metaphors, a teammate should be polite, but **assertive,** stating his or her position. The copilot might **advocate,** "Captain, I'm uncomfortable with this approach. I think it would be safer to go around and try again." This communication strategy keeps all team members focused on the safe completion of the team's task.

Fifth, communication should be used *to establish leadership* roles. Since the *TRM* model is a decentralized approach to leadership, it is important conflicts be surfaced to avoid a *groupthink* environment discussed in chapter two. In this more open environment, leaders do not shy away from conflict, but actively work to surface it as a learning opportunity. In addition, the leader strives to support a climate where uncertainties and complexities of group process can be explored. Being aware of a group's tendency to scapegoat, the successful leader is willing to take action when warranted to redirect group antagonism, including having the nerve to say the hard thing and tolerate uncertainty. Finally, a leader understands his or her "role" and manages personal and professional boundaries in a manner that builds trust within the team. By using one's emotional intelligence and instincts, a leader can uncover many of the covert activities that debilitate teams and organizations, sabotaging change efforts.

III. Sense-Making

Sense making is the process of constructing a mental map of current events by evaluating one's perception of reality 'outside' through what one is experiencing inside. Although this may seem simple, Karl Weick reminds us that sense making in organizational life presents "puzzling terrain" because groups "lend themselves to multiple, conflicting interpretations, all of which are plausible."[161] Given the multitude of conflicting interpretations and the time urgency of some decision making scenarios in technical fields like aviation, medicine or law enforcement, how can we become more efficient sense-makers?

First, we must *identify the correct problem*, remaining vigilantly *curious* about others, ourselves and our environment *gathering information* to help keep our perceptions as closely aligned to reality as possible. Making assumptions is risky business. As we *analyze* this information we naturally attempt to create order—to make sense—within our mind.

For example, perhaps a co-worker snapped at us when chatting at the water cooler. "He must be angry with me over the latest project assignments" or "she has always hated people who look like me." It is easy to jump to conclusions as we attempt to assign meaning quickly and therefore stop processing the situation. Once we understand it, we think we can forget it or, better yet, use this piece of meaning to make sense out of something else, building a house-of-*false reality*-cards. The longer we can *tolerate ambiguity*, and sit with the uncertainty of a situation, the longer we can remain curious, gathering important information in order to make a reality based assessment.

We can avoid the house-of-*false reality*-cards trap by routinely *cross-checking* what is inside our head and bodies with the outside world, without making presumptions about meaning. For instance, did I just yell at a co-worker because it was warranted or because I never thought she deserved that promotion anyway? Am I feeling short-fused because it's almost lunch time and I'm hungry or is this project really falling apart?

Once we have gathered information, resisting our urge to jump to conclusions by tolerating the ambiguity of this experience, and cross-checked information to ensure it's accurate, it is time to *develop a plan* to provide a temporary guide for action. I say temporary because one should continue the sense making cycle of gathering and cross-checking, *modifying the plan as required* as new realities emerge.

Obviously, given the time constraints of some challenges in high-risk teams, the sense making cycle may be quite short. In this case, the time critical nature of the situation requires a more *centralized leadership* approach, clear direction from a central source. But in most cases, there is more time than one initially believes to make sense of a situation. For instance, even when pilots are confronted by an engine fire in flight, clearly one of the most hazardous emergencies, they are still trained to refer to a checklist, confirm the presence and exact location of the fire with fellow aircrew. Before securing the burning engine, they confirm that they have their hand on the correct selector before moving any switches or levers. Although this may take a minute or two, history has shown more than a few pilots have shut down the good engine in flight in a confused state of sense making. It is often the inability to tolerate ambiguity as important facts become clear that forces teams to make mistakes.

IV. Team Work

Good *teamwork* can be thought of as the successful integration of the three TRM elements: leadership, communication and sense-making. TRM supports a more decentralized leadership strategy where teammates can share the leadership tasks, assigning duties based on skill not job title. By communicating openly and professionally, without inappropriate jokes or confusing jargon, using common communication strategies such as '*CUS*' *words* and *The Big Three,* teams can create an environment where a successful exchange of information can occur, establishing predictable behavior patterns and maintaining attention to the task, essential to *teamwork* in high-risk environments.

How can we assess the effectiveness of *teamwork* in high-risk groups? I propose that one evaluate three areas of high-risk team performance: decision-making, workload management and error management. First, observe how decisions are made within the team or organization. Is input solicited from a variety of areas or are decisions made by one person, behind closed doors with little feedback from outside? Second, assess the manner in which the workload is managed. Are tasks solely the responsibility of certain individuals or is everyone *authorized* to pitch in and help, when required? Conversely, are individuals allowed to become saturated by the extent of their workload while others sit idly by? Finally, how are the inevitable human errors managed within the team or organization? Is it assumed that some errors will naturally occur or is there pressure to achieve an unattainable level of perfection? When errors are made, are individuals scapegoated?

An excellent example of *teamwork* within a high-risk organization is Southwest Airlines. Southwest management fosters a corporate culture where employees can have fun and be themselves. This culture encourages *leadership* by delegating responsibility, empowering employees to make decisions as 'the experts' in their work area. When a Southwest 737 pulls into the gate, employees *communicate* and coordinate activates in order to get the airplane 'turned around' and out on time—usually within twenty minutes. That means pilots may unload baggage, flight attendants may load cases of soda and peanuts, and gate agents may clean newspapers and trash off the passengers seats. No one needs to be told to help out, as a team they *make sense* of the situation and develop a plan after evaluating the tasks that need to be accomplished. As a result, the team balances the workload to achieve their goal: the twenty minute turnaround.

CHAPTER VII

▼

THE 'TEMPORARY ORGANIZATION'

 LEARNING OBJECTIVES

1. Describe the *primary task* of the group dynamics workshop.
2. Explain the event's structure and the concept behind the 'temporary organization.'
3. Identify participants' role within the *experiential learning* format.
4. Identify the role of staff within the group dynamics workshop.

Introduction

The previous six chapters provided foundational information, preparing participants for the *experiential learning* phase of the program you will soon embark upon. As staff and members build this 'temporary organization' together, the workshop will develop its own dynamics, rituals, myths and fantasies, as ways of working within its structure emerge, creating the larger organizational culture. Although many of the concepts discussed in the previous chapters may be present within this event, this *Primer* is not meant to provide a 'checklist of group dynamics.' Instead, by engaging participants in the examination and interpretation of these dynamics and rituals, the workshop provides opportunities for participants and staff to learn about themselves and their own reactions to ambiguity, change, anxiety and stress as well as that of those around them. Try to pay attention to these signals.

There are no right or wrong answers. This exp*eriential* workshop provides opportunities to learn what *you* choose to learn. Each person is encouraged to use his or her own *authority* to accept what is useful learning and reject what is not. By examining what is going on as it occurs in the 'here-and-now' of workshop events in the 'temporary organization,' participants are offered opportunities to apply and reflect on similar experiences in their outside organizational life.

Primary Task

The *Primary Task* of this group dynamics workshop is:

> *To study the exercise of leadership, authority and teamwork through the group dynamics that emerge between and among workshop participants and staff within the 'temporary organization' these groups build together.*

As a result, all behaviors—staff and participant alike—will be open for interpretation.

Workshop events begin in the morning and end in the evening, just like the schedule of many work organizations. There will be scheduled events with different tasks and roles, and variable sized groups, as in most organizations. Some groups will seem large, similar to the size of an organization's annual retreat, military squadron or town hall meeting. Large groups can feel chaotic, unorganized, and even frightening. Other groups will be smaller, and can therefore feel safer, more intimate and familiar to some people, such as a department, family or athletic team. Try to pay attention to these dynamics and how *you* feel in these various group and 'work' settings.

There will be breaks between events when participants will have informal opportunities to meet with others—or not—as in a regular workday. How does this time get used? Just as in 'real organizations,' does it seem that most of the 'real work' seems to get done between events—at the water cooler or coffee pot, in the restroom or over lunch, on the golf course or racquet ball court? Or do important issues surface during scheduled meetings when everyone is present?

'Learning from Experience'—The Event's Format

The workshop aims to draw participants from diverse work settings and roles, many from high-risk organizations such as military, aviation, law enforcement, and fire fighting. Although nothing is 'taught,' people often find that the 'temporary organization' that staff and participants create together mirrors patterns and relationships in their daily work lives. Anyone who has a serious commitment to learning more about the dynamics of leadership, authority, and groups in organizational life is encouraged to attend. Participation is the key because what you learn from this experience is unique and may be applied to the roles you take up in your own organizations and networks.

Experiential learning can be intense. Participants who are ill or experiencing an unusual amount of personal stress may wish to forgo attendance at this time.

The Role of Staff

Staff have several roles within the group dynamics workshop:

First, they collectively act as management of the 'temporary organization' that is being built through staff-participant collaboration. As a result, the Executive Director and her team take responsibility and authority to provide the boundary conditions—time, task, territory and role—necessary so that all participants can engage with the primary task of the event. How effectively do staff accomplish this task?

Second, individual staff members take up a variety of specific consultancy roles throughout the event. For example, although the Executive

Director takes up a *formal authority role* in relationship to the entire group dynamics workshop, she will participate in a number of different group events taking up a different role in each under the under the supervision of the 'Director' of that sub-system. In other words, just like the CEO of Microsoft may take up a different role when in a working meeting with software engineers, roles within the 'temporary organization' are also situation and group specific. How well does the Executive Director hold her authority, manage boundaries, contain anxiety and balance roles?

Staff members assigned to consultant roles within group events will be working on the primary task of the event, offering working hypothesis based on their understanding of what is happening in the 'here-and-now'. In other words, based on their own experiences, feelings and observations of the event, they will offer an interpretation of what is 'really' going on. These observations may be subjective and participants are free to accept or reject the validity of these hypothesis based on their own authority and encouraged to share their experiences of what is occurring.

As a result, staff are not innocent bystanders or observers but active participants in the *learning struggle* to make sense of, and be heard within, the emerging 'temporary organization.' How well do staff accomplish this task?

Workshop Events

The group dynamics workshop will consist of *experiential* events selected from among the following (Not all workshops include the same combinations.):

Opening Event

The workshop begins with a *plenary* session or full meeting of all event participants, providing an opportunity to introduce staff and participants and the experiential learning methods to be used through out. This plenary offers staff and participants the chance to continue the process of 'crossing the boundary' as they begin building the 'temporary organization' together.

Small Group

Staff and participants are assigned by the Executive Director to attend a Small Group Event. Similar in size to a small department, family, team or work group, this event is designed to offer opportunities to study the dynamics that arise in the 'here-and-now' of small group life. By keeping groups small, participants have the opportunity to explore their face-to-face interpersonal relations as they occur in real time.

Large Group

All workshop participants and select members of staff will attend the Large Group Event. Similar in size to an organizational retreat, large board meeting, military unit or town hall gathering, this event offers opportunities to study the dynamics that arise in the 'here-and-now' of large group life.

For example, large groups often instill a sense of chaos and uncontained emotions leading to splits within the group membership as sub-groups emerge based upon fantasy and myth. Examining the emergence of identities, alliances, loyalties and feuds provides opportunity to explore dynamics common in most organizations as whole.

By juxtapositioning large and small group events throughout the workshop, participants are offered the opportunity to explore their own comforts and anxieties, and that of their fellow participants, in various group settings. In which setting do you feel most comfortable?

Observed Staff Meeting[162]

The Observed Staff Meeting provides workshop participants an opportunity to observe Directors and their teams working in public as they engage with the workshop's primary task. Similar to a staff meeting which you might find in any organization, this event offers people a chance to increase their understanding of the dynamics of leadership, authority and teamwork that are emerging within the 'temporary organization' being built.

Collaborative Event[163]

All staff and workshop participants will be involved in the Collaborative Event. This event provides opportunities for the study of organizational processes—the overt and covert dynamics that can enhance or undermine one's ability to collaborate—as participants attempt to work creatively on a common task.

> The *primary task* of the Collaborative Event is for workshop participants to plan and create an 'event' or 'product' to take place during the session described as 'open time' in the schedule of events and to explore the *dynamics of collaboration* as they occur in this process.

Workshop participants will:

- Collaborate to create an 'event' or 'product' which can be offered within the boundaries of the open time in the workshop schedule. Examples might be a performance such as a play, dance or sporting event, an artistic display of pictures, stories or poems, a product or a training session;

- Communicate to the Executive Director and her management team by an established time the suitability and tastefulness of this 'product' or 'event' for an educational workshop such as this; and

- Develop a sufficient organizational structure by which to manage this event.

Given these three steps are sufficiently accomplished, the Executive Director will temporarily turn over management of the workshop to the participants' Management Team to host the event within the boundaries of the open time in the workshop schedule. At this time, the staff group will temporarily become conference members and can take up roles accordingly.

The staff group will form a sub-group and be working openly throughout the Collaborative Event. Staff continue to functioning as collective management and as consultants, and are therefore available for collaboration and consultation. Although the staff group is managing the event, they are not managing group members or how they undertake their task.

Application Group

Staff and participants are assigned by the Executive Director to attend the Application Group. The task of this event is twofold: First, these groups provide participants the opportunity to reflect about their workshop experiences in order to examine the various roles they have taken up within the events; Second, the group assists participants in relating these experiences to the roles they will resume in their lives outside the workshop.

Closing Plenary

The workshop concludes with a closing plenary, offering participants a chance to reflect in public about their workshop experience as they prepare to cross the boundary back to the outside world. Upon the conclusion of this event the 'temporary organization' will be disbanded and the Executive Director and her staff will no longer be in role.

Summary

This chapter provided important contextual information for participants preparing to enter the *experiential learning* phase of the program. By understanding the design and primary task of workshop events, participants can understand better the dynamics occurring around them. Yet, this chapter is not meant to provide a 'checklist of group dynamics.' Instead, it is an invitation to explore the dynamics of the 'temporary organization' as staff and participants build it together.

CHAPTER VIII

▼

HIGH-RISK TEAMS AT WORK

Professionals working in high-risk industries such as aviation, automotive technology, emergency planning, engineering, medicine, firefighting, law enforcement, military, nuclear power and off-shore drilling, among others, know that there are a number of unique dynamics, which they must manage in order to perform their jobs effectively and safely. Balancing these complex dynamics such as time urgency, peer pressure, exposure to personal risk, professional competitiveness, interpersonal conflicts, reputation management and living with the weighty repercussions of one's decisions is a daily part of high-risk teams' operations. Yet, the culture in many high-risk organizations emphasizes technical training instead of leadership and team-building skills, assuming these latter skills employees will pick up 'on the job' as they rise though the organizational ranks. This does not always occur effectively. As a result, a new training program is needed for high-risk teams.

The previous chapters provided the background, theories and methods of a new team training model designed specifically for high-risk organizations, called *Team Resource Management (TRM)*. *TRM* **is a sense-making process designed to expose and manage team errors and conflicts as they shape *authority* relations in a dynamic context.** Central to the *TRM* model are the assumptions that people behave differently in different groups and that team dynamics often move in unpredictably complex—not reliably linear—ways. Unlike other team training models, *TRM* refocuses the level of analysis on the covert group processes, the often unspoken dynamics of the group, which operate not at the level of individual distinctions, but at the level of the *group-as-a-whole*. By identifying and assessing both obvious and not-so-obvious influences on team performance, *TRM* can help overcome obstacles to effective teamwork, reducing errors and miscommunications in high-risk industries.

As a result, two leadership strategies become clear: First, successful high-risk teams need people who can identify, confront and vent anxieties, rather than becoming debilitated by them, and either thoughtlessly jumping to action or seeking to scapegoat; Second, high-risk organizations need to develop a more inclusive culture that accepts complexity, tolerates ambiguity, surfaces conflicts and supports a learning process at all levels in order to manage organizational anxiety. Although the essential elements of the *TRM* model are described in this *Primer*, *TRM* is not something one learns only by reading about it. Like any new skill, the tools it helps build must be put into practice so that team members can develop appropriate mastery.

I invite participants to explore group dynamics and test their *TRM* skills in a number of experiential exercises. Be curious, have fun and explore leadership and teambuilding as we develop a 'temporary organization' together.

Selected Bibliography

Interested in learning more about group dynamics, leadership and the Tavistock method? Here are a few suggestions, in alphabetical order:

➢ Banet, A. G., & Hayden, C. (1977). A Tavistock primer. *The 1977 Annual Handbook for Group Facilitators*, (pp. 155-167). San Diego, CA: University Associates.

➢ Bion, W. R. (1961). *Experiences in groups.* London: Routledge.

➢ Fraher, A. L. (2004). *A history of group study and psychodynamic organizations.* London: Free Association Books.

➢ French, R., & Vince, R. (1999). *Group relations, management, and organization.* New York: Oxford University Press.

➢ Gabriel, Y. (1999). *Organizations in depth.* Thousand Oaks, CA: Sage.

➢ Hirschhorn, L. (1988). *The workplace within: Psychodynamics of organizational life.* Cambridge, MA: The MIT Press.

➢ Menzies, I. E. P. (1959). The functioning of social systems as a defense against anxiety: A report on a study of the nursing service of a general hospital. *Human Relations*, 13, 95-121.

➢ Miller, E. (1993). *From dependency to autonomy: Studies in organization and change.* London: Free Association Books.

➢ Obholzer, A., & Roberts, V. Z. (Eds.) (1994). *The unconscious at work.* London: Routledge.

➢ Rice, A. K. (1965). *Learning for leadership.* London: Tavistock Publications Limited.

➤ Smith, K., & Berg, D. (1987). *Paradoxes of group life.* San Francisco: Jossey-Bass.

Relevant Journals

> An Organization for Promoting Understanding of Society (OPUS): www.opus.org.uk *Human Relations*, published by the Tavistock Institute and Sage. http://www.tavinstitute.org/hrindex.htm
> *Organisational & Social Dynamics,* published by An Organization for Promoting Understanding of Society (OPUS) and Karnac books. www.opus.org.uk

Relevant Websites

> A.K. Rice Institute for the Study of Social Systems: www.akriceinstitute.org
> *Grex*: www.grex.info
> The International Society for the Psychoanalytic Study of Organizations (ISPSO): www.ispso.org
> The Tavistock Institute: www.tavinstitute.org

References

Banet, A. G., & Hayden, C. (1977). A Tavistock primer. *The 1977 Annual Handbook for Group Facilitators,* (pp. 155-167). San Diego, CA: University Associates.

Bion, W. R. (1961). *Experiences in groups.* London: Routledge.

Bion, W. R., & Rickman, J. (1943). Intra-group tensions in therapy. *The Lancet,* 2, 678-681.

Birnbach, R. A & Longridge, T. M. (1993). The regulatory perspective. In E. L. Wiener, B. G. Kanki, and R. L. Helmreich (Eds.). *Cockpit Resource Management.* San Diego: Academic Press. 263-282.

Blake, R. R. & Mouton, J. (1964). *The managerial grid.* Houston: Gulf Press.

Bradford, L. P., Gibb, J. R., & Benne, K. D. (1964). *T-Group Theory and Laboratory Method.* New York: John Wiley & Sons.

Brady, T. (2000). Pilot education: The beginnings. *The Journal of Aviation/Aerospace Education & Research,* 9(2), 21-25.

Broder, J. M. (2005, July 29) Police chiefs moving to share terror data. *The New York Times,* p. A12.

Burns, J. M. (1978). *Leadership.* New York: Harper & Row Publishers.

Cherniss, C. (2000). Social and emotional competence in the workplace. In R. Bar-On and J. D. A. Parker (Eds.). *The handbook of emotional intelligence.* San Francisco: Jossey-Bass. 433-458.

Churchman, C. W. (1968). *The systems approach.* New York: Dell Publishing.

Cook, G. N. (1995). Cockpit resource management training: Are current instructional methods likely to be successful? *The Journal of Aviation/Aerospace Education Research,* 7(2), 26-34.

Conger, J. A. (1993). Personal growth training: Snake oil or pathway to leadership. *Organizational Dynamics,* 22(1), 19-30.

Federal Aviation Administration (2004). Crew resource management training (AC-120-51E).

Flin, R. H. (1995). Crew resource management for teams in the offshore oil industry. *Journal of European Industrial Training,* 19(9), 23-27.

Follett, M. P. (1996). The giving of orders. In J. M. Shafritz and J. S. Ott (Eds.). *Classics of organization theory,* 4th edition. New York: Harcourt Brace College Publishers.

Fraher, A. L. (2004a). *A history of group study and psychodynamic organizations.* London: Free Association Books.

Fraher, A. L. (2004b). Flying the Friendly Skies: Why U.S. Commercial Airline Pilots Want To Carry Guns. *Human Relations.* 57(5), 573-595.

Fraher, A. L. (2004c). Systems Psychodynamics: The Formative Years of an Interdisciplinary Field at the Tavistock Institute. *History of Psychology,* 7(1), 65-84.

Fraher, A. L. (2005) Team Resource Management (TRM): A Tavistock Approach to Leadership in High-Risk Environments. *Organisational and Social Dynamics,* 5(2), 163-182.

Gabriel, Y. (1999). *Organizations in depth.* Thousand Oaks, CA: Sage.

George, J. M. (2000). Emotions and leadership: The role of emotional intelligence. *Human Relations,* 53(8), 1027-1055.

Ginnett, R. C. (1993). Crews as groups: Their formation and their leadership. In E. L. Wiener, B. G. Kanki, and R. L. Helmreich (Eds.). *Cockpit Resource Management.* San Diego: Academic Press. 71-98.

Goleman, D. (1995). *Emotional intelligence: Why it can matter more than IQ.* New York: Bantam Books.

Goleman, D. (1998). *Working with emotional intelligence.* New York: Bantam Books.

Gould, L. (1997). Correspondences between Bion's basic assumption theory and Klein's developmental positions: An outline. *Free Associations,* 7(1), 15-30.

Gould, L. Stapley, L. F. & Stein, M. (Eds.). (2001). *The systems psychodynamics of organizations.* New York: Karnac, 2001.

Heifetz, R. A. (1994). *Leadership without easy answers*. Cambridge, Mass: The Belknap Press of Harvard University Press.

Heifetz, R. A., & Laurie, D. L. (1997). The work of leadership. *Harvard Business Review*, January-February, 124-134.

Helmreich, R. L. & Foushee, C. (1993). Why crew resource management? Empirical and theoretical bases of human factors training in aviation. In E. L. Wiener, B. G. Kanki, and R. L. Helmreich (Eds.). *Cockpit Resource Management*. San Diego: Academic Press. 1-41.

Helmreich, R. L., Merritt, A. C., & Wilhelm, J. A. (1999). The evolution of Crew Resource Management training in commercial aviation. *International Journal of Aviation Psychology*, 9(1), 19-32.

Hershey, P., & Blanchard, K. H. (1993). *Management of organizational behavior*. Englewood Cliffs, NJ: Prentice Hall.

Hirschhorn, L. (1988). *The workplace within: Psychodynamics of organizational life*. Cambridge, MA: The MIT Press.

Hirschhorn, L. (1997). *Reworking authority: Leading and following in the post-modern organisation*. Cambridge, MA: The MIT Press.

Hirshhorn, L. (1999). Leaders and followers. In Y. Gabriel, *Organizations in depth. London: Sage Publications*. 139-165.

Hughes, R. L., Ginnett, R. C., & Curphy, G. J. (1996). *Leadership: Enhancing the lessons of experience*. Chicago: Irwin.

Janis, I. (1972). *Victims of groupthink*. Boston: Houghton Mifflin.

Jaques, E. (1952). *The changing culture of a factory*. New York: Dryden Press, Inc.

Jones, K. B. (1993). *Compassionate authority: Democracy and the representation of women.*. New York: Routledge.

Kanki, B. G., & Palmer, M. T. (1993). Communication and crew resource management. In In E. L. Wiener, B. G. Kanki, and R. L. Helmreich (Eds.). *Cockpit Resource Management*. San Diego: Academic Press. 99-136.

Kern, T. (2001). *Controlling pilot error: Culture, environment, & CRM*. New York: McGraw-Hill.

Klein, E. B. & Astrachan, B. M. (1971). Learning in groups: a comparison of study group and t-groups. *The Journal of Applied Behavioral Science, 7*(6), 659-683.

Krause, S. S. (2003). *Aircraft safety: Accident investigations, analyses and applications* (2nd Ed.). New York: McGraw-Hill.

Levi, D. (2001). *Group dynamics for teams*. Thousand Oaks, CA: Sage Publishers.

Mayer, J. D., Salovey, P., & Caruso, D. R. (2000). Emotional intelligence as zeitgeist, as personality, and as a mental ability. In R. Bar-On and J. D. A. Parker (Eds.). *The handbook of emotional intelligence*. San Francisco: Jossey-Bass. 92-117.

Mayo, E. (1933). *The human problems of an industrial civilization*. New York: The Viking Press.

McGregor, W. (1960). *The human side of enterprise*. New York: McGraw Hill.

Mearns, K., Flin, R., & O'Connor, P. (2001). Sharing 'worlds of risk'; improving communications with crew resource management. *Journal of Risk Research, 4*(4), 377-392.

Menzies, I. E. P. (1959). The functioning of social systems as a defense against anxiety: A report on a study of the nursing service of a general hospital. *Human Relations, 13*, 95-121.

Miller, E. J. (1989). *The Leicester model: Experiential study of group and organizational processes*. TIHR Occasional Paper No. 10. London: The Tavistock Institute of Human Relations.

Miller, E. (1993). *From dependency to autonomy: Studies in organization and change*. London: Free Association Books.

Miller, E. J., & Rice, A. K. (1967). *Systems of organization*. London: Tavistock Publications Limited.

Musson, D. M., & Helmreich, R. L. (2004). Team training and resource management in health care: Current issues and future directions. *Harvard Health Policy Review, 5*(1), 25-35.

Neumann, J. E., Holvino, E., & Braxton, E. T. (2004). Evolving a third way to group consultancy: Bridging two models of theory and practice.

In S. Cytrynbaum and D. A. Noumair (Eds.) *Group Relations Reader 3.* Jupiter, FL: A. K. Rice Institute. 383-402.

Phillips, G. M., Pedersen, D. J., & Wood, J. T. (1979). *Group discussion: A practical guide to participation and leadership.* Boston: Houghton Mifflin Company.

Rice, A. K. (1965). *Learning for leadership.* London: Tavistock Publications Limited.

Roach, C. F. & Behling, O. (1984). Functionalism: Basis for an alternate approach to the study of leadership. In J. G. Hunt, D. M. Hosking, C. A. Schriesheim, & R. Stewart (Eds.), *Leaders and managers: International perspectives on managerial behavior and leadership.* Elmsford, NY: Pergamon.

Rosenbaum, M. (1976). Group psychotherapy. In M. Rosenbaum & A. Snadowsky (Eds.), *The intensive group experience.* New York: The Free Press.

Rost, J. (1991). *Leadership for the twenty-first century.* Westport, CT: Praeger.

Ruffell Smith, H. P. (1979). A simulator study of the interaction of pilot workload with errors, vigilance, and decisions (NASA technical memo 78482). Moffett Field, CA: NASA Ames Research Center.

Schwartz, H. S. (1987). On the psychodynamics of organizational disaster: The case of the space shuttle Challenger. *Columbia Journal of World Business.,*

Schwartz, H. S. (1989). Organizational disaster and organizational decay: The case of the National Aeronautics and Space Administration. *Industrial Crisis Quarterly,* 3. 319-334.

Shafritz, J. M. & and Ott, J. S. (Eds.). (1996). *Classics of organization theory,* 4th ed. New York: Harcourt Brace College Publishers.

Shepard, B. (2000). *A war of nerves.* London: Pimlico.

Smith, K., & Berg, D. (1987). *Paradoxes of group life.* San Francisco: Jossey-Bass.

Smith, K. K., Simmons, V. M., & Thames, T. B. (1989). "Fix the women": An intervention into an organizational conflict based on parallel process thinking. *Journal of Applied Behavioral Science,* 25(1), 11-29.

Stacey, R. (2001). Complexity at the 'edge' of the basic assumption group. In L. Gould, L. F. Stapley, & M. Stein (Eds.), *The systems psychodynamics of organizations*. London: Karnac Books. 91-114.

Trist, E. (1993). Introduction to volume II. In E. Trist & H. Murray (Eds.), *The social engagement of social science: A Tavistock anthology, volume II: The socio-technical perspective*. Philadelphia: University of Pennsylvania Press. 36-60.

Trist, E. (1985). Working with Bion in the 1940s: The group decade. In M. Pines (Ed.), *Bion and group psychotherapy*. London: Routledge & Kegan Paul. 1-46.

Trist, E. & Murray, H. (1990). Historical overview: The foundation and development of the Tavistock Institute to 1989. In E. Trist & H. Murray (Eds.), *The social engagement of social science, volume I: The socio-psychological perspective* (pp. 1-36). Philadelphia: University of Pennsylvania Press.

Trist, E. L. & C. Sofer (1959). *Exploration in group relations*. Leicester: Leicester University Press.

Tuckman, B. & Jensen, M. (1977). Stages of small group development revisited. *Group and Organizational Studies, 2*, 419-427.

Turquet, P. M. (1974). Leadership: The individual and the group. In G. S. Gibbard, J. J. Hartman, & R. D. Mann, (Eds.), *Analysis of groups* (pp. 349-386). San Francisco: Jossey-Bass Publishers.

United Airlines. (2003). *Flight Operations Manual*.

Weick, K. E. (2001). *Making sense of the organization*. Oxford: Blackwell Publishing.

Weiner, E. L., Kanki, B. G., & Helmreich, R. L. (1993). (Eds.). *Cockpit Resource Management*. San Diego: Academic Press.

Weitzel, T. R. & Lehrer, H. R. (1992) A turning point in aviation training: The AQP mandates crew resource management and line operational simulations. *The Journal of Aviation/Aerospace education & Research, 3*(1), 14-20.

Wilson, A. T. M. (1950). *The Tavistock Institute of Human Relations: Development and work 1946-1950*. London: Tavistock Publications.

NOTES

1 See Fraher, 2005 for more information about the development of TRM.

2 For our purposes, a high-risk team is two or more people working together in an environment where there is significant risk of injury or death to themselves or to others as a result of their performance.

3 For instance, Flin, 1995; Fraher, 2004a, 2004b, 2005; Kern 2001; Krause, 2003; Mearns, Flin and O'Connor, 2001; Weiner, Kanki, and Helmreich, 1993.

4 Mearns, Flin and O'Connor, 2001, p. 378.

5 This is more formally referred to as the field of *systems psychodynamics*. See Fraher, 2004c; Gould, Stapley & Stein, 2001.

6 Broder, 2005, *New York Times*, p. A12.

7 George, 2000, p. 1043.

8 Cherniss, 2000, p. 434.

9 Goleman, 1995, p. 34; 1998.

10 Ibid.

11 Mayer, Salovey, and Caruso, 2000, p. 93.

12 Goleman, 1995, p. 34; 1998.

13 Emphasis added; Cherniss, 2000, p. 450.

14 Ibid.

15 In particular, encounter groups, T-groups and sensitivity training made famous by the National Training Laboratories in the 1950s, '60s and 70s.

16 The Tavistock Institute of Human Relations, 30 Tabernacle Street, London EC2A 4UE, www.tavinstitute.org

17 Miller, 1989; Fraher, 2004a, 2004c.

18 Banet and Hayden, 1977, p. 156.

19 Ibid.

21 Rice, 1965.

[22] George, 2000, p. 1028.

[23] Critique offered by K. B. Jones in chapter 3, *Compassionate Authority: Democracy and the Representation of Women*, Routledge, 1993.

[24] Mayo, 1933.

[25] McGregor, 1960. Hershey and Blanchard, 1993.

[26] McGregor, 1960, p. 179.

[27] Burns, 1978; Rost, 1991

[28] Hughes, Ginnett, and Curphy, 1996; Roach and Behling, 1984.

[29] Hirschhorn, 1999, p. 141 cites Zaleznik, 1989.

[30] Ibid.

[31] Ibid, p. 142.

[32] Heifetz, 1994, p. 57.

[33] Oliver Stone, 1986, released by Hemdale Film Corp.

[34] Captain Ahab is the monomaniacal sea captain in the classic tale *Moby Dick*, whose single-minded pursuit of the colossal white whale who took his leg resulted in the loss of ship and crew. In the story, Moby Dick came to represent all that's evil as Ahab's need for revenge propelled the sailors to disaster.

[35] Levi, 2001.

[36] Ibid, pp. 175-6.

[37] Emphasis added, Smith and Berg, 1987, p. 66.

[38] Ibid.

[39] Ibid, p. 68.

[40] Ibid, p. 70-71.

[41] Gabriel, 1999, p. 67.

[42] Phillips, Pedersen and Wood,1979, p. 53.

[43] Levi, 2001, p. 163; Phillips, Pedersen and Wood,1979, p. 53; Janis, 1972.

[44] Schwartz, 1989, p. 324.

[45] Schwartz, 1987, 1989.

[46] Gabriel, 1999, p. 81.

[47] Weick, 2001, p. 9.

[48] Bion, 1961.

[49] Ibid, p. 74, 82, 99.

[50] Ibid; Gabriel, 1999.

[51] Ibid, p. 63, 65.

[52] Ibid, p. 135.

[53] Turquet, 1974, p. 364.

[54] Ibid, p. 365.

[55] Ibid, p. 367.

[56] Gould, 1997, p. 22.

[57] Miller and Rice, 1967.

[58] Cited in Miller, 1993, p. 10.

[59] Ibid, p. 11.

[60] Ibid.

[61] 1993.

[62] 1965.

[63] Rice, 1965, p. 11.

[64] Ibid.

[65] Miller, 1993, p. 19.

[66] Rice, 1965, p. 11.

[67] Bion, 1961; Gabriel, 1999; Miller, 1993.

[68] Rice, 1965, p. 17.

[69] Ibid, p. 18.

[70] 1988, 1999.

[71] Hirschhorn, 1999, p. 145-146.

[72] Heifetz and Laurie, 1997, p. 127.

[73] Ibid.

[74] Ibid; Heifetz, 1994.

[75] Fraher, 2004a.

[76] Helmreich and Foushee, 1993, p. 5.

[77] Cook, 1995; Weiner, Kanki, and Helmreich, 1993; Wetzel and Lehrer, 1992.

[78] Helmreich and Foushee, 1993, p. 7.

[79] Brady, 2000, p. 22.

[80] Ginnett, 1993, p. 72.

[81] Birnbach and Longridge, 1993, p. 265.

[82] Emphasis added, Helmreich and Foushee, 1993, p. 5.

[83] Krause, 2003, p. 138.

[84] Weiner, Kanki, and Helmreich, 1993, p. xvii.

[85] H.P. Ruffell Smith, 1979.

[86] Emphasis added; Krause, 2003, p. 210.

[87] NTSB Report DCA79AA005, 1978.

[88] For example see Flin, 1995; Mearns, Flin and O'Connor, 2001; Musson and Helmreich, 2004.

[89] Helmreich, Merritt, and Wilhelm, 1999, p. 19.

[90] Cook, 1995.

[91] Conger, 1993, p. 22.

[92] Ibid, p. 23.

[93] Italics added; Helmreich, Merritt, and Wilhelm, 1999, p. 20.

[94] Blake and Mouton, 1964.

[95] Bradford Gibb and Benne, 1964, p. 16.

[96] Conger, 1993, p. 22.

[97] Bradford, Gibb and Benne, 1964, p. 18-20.

[98] Ibid, p. 25.

[99] Ibid, p. 18.

[100] Cook, 1985.

[101] For more information about Tavistock history, theories and methods, see optional course textbook available online or at Miramar bookstore: Fraher, A. L. (2004). *A history of group study and psychodynamic organizations*. London: Free Association Books.

[102] British 'public' schools would be equivalent to American 'private' schools.

[103] Approximately 9% of the officers and 4% of the enlisted ranks had broken down as a result of the fighting near the Flemish town of Ypres in December 1914 (Shepard, 2000, p. 21).

[104] Ibid, p. 30.

[105] Trist, 1985, p. 13.

[106] Fraher, 2004a.

[107] Trist and Murray, 1990.

[108] Rosenbaum, 1976, p. 27.

[109] Trist, 1985, p. 30.

[110] Ibid, p. 31.

[111] Emphasis added; Gabriel, 1999, p. 118.

[112] Fraher, 2004a, 2004c.

[113] Trist, 1985, p. 15.

114 Wilson "in memoriam" brochure, December 7, 1978, p. 5. Tavistock Institute archives.

115 Wilson, 1950, p. 5.

116 E. Miller, personal communication, September 30, 2001.

117 Trist and Sofer, 1959, p. 5.

118 Miller, 1989, p. 2

119 Bion and Rickman, 1943.

120 Fraher, 2004a, 2004c.

121 Fraher, 2004a; Miller, 1993; Neumann, Holvino and Braxton, 2004.

122 Fraher, 2004a.

123 Fraher, 2004a; Klein and Astrachan, 1971; Neumann, Holvino and Braxton, 2004.

124 Tuckman and Jensen, 1977; Levi, 2001, p. 41.

125 See www.amazon.com.

126 Federal Aviation Administration AC 120-51E, p. 4.

127 See Fraher, 2005 for more information about the development of TRM.

128 Fraher, 2004a, 2004c; Trist, 1993.

129 Trist, 1993, p. 36.

130 Follett, 1996, p. 158.

131 Mayo, 1933.

132 Emphasis added; Shafritz and Ott, 1996, p. 150-151.

133 Mayo, 1933, p. 1.

134 Trist, 1993, p. 38.

135 Obituary: *The Times*, June 18, 1993; *The Independent*, June 14, 1993. Tavistock Institute archives.

136 Smith and Berg, 1987, p. 63.

137 Fraher, 2004a.

138 Miller, 1993, p. 19.

139 Emphasis added, Rice, 1965, p. 11.

140 Stacey, 2001.

141 Emphasis added, Smith, Simmons and Thames, 1989, p. 11.

142 Ibid, p. 16.

143 Ibid, p. 19.

144 Ibid.

[145] Ibid, p. 18.

[146] Ibid, p. 20.

[147] Krause, 2003, p. 3.

[148] Called *Navigating Change,* the goal of the training was "to provide pilots in leadership positions with useful information that may help them assist others who have concerns or problems with gender/minority issues" (United Airlines, personal correspondence, January 10, 2001.)

[149] United Airlines, 1999, *Navigating Change* training materials, p. H10.

[150] Emphasis added, Churchman, 1968, p. 240.

[151] Jaques, 1952; Menzies, 1959.

[152] Menzies, 1959, p. 101.

[153] Hirshhorn, 1988; Gabriel, 1999, p. 225.

[154] Fraher, 2004b.

[155] Hirshhorn, 1988; Gabriel, 1999, p. 225.

[156] United Airlines, Flight Operations Manual, 2003, p. 36.20.7

[157] Kanki and Palmer, 1993, p. 99.

[158] Levi, 2001, p. 96.

[159] United Airlines, Flight Operations Manual, 2003, p. 36.20.7

[160] Kanki and Palmer, 1993, p. 112.

[161] Weick, 2001, p. 9.

[162] This event is based on the work of Terri Monroe.

[163] This event is based on the work of Zanne Lorenzen and Karen Izod.

INDEX

978-0-595-37739-8
0-595-37739-4

Printed in the United States
79510LV00006B/217